OECD Studies on Water

Making Blended Finance Work for Water and Sanitation

UNLOCKING COMMERCIAL FINANCE FOR SDG 6

OECD

BETTER POLICIES FOR BETTER LIVES

Please cite this publication as:
OECD (2019), *Making Blended Finance Work for Water and Sanitation: Unlocking Commercial Finance for SDG 6*, OECD Studies on Water, OECD Publishing, Paris, *https://doi.org/10.1787/5efc8950-en*.

ISBN 978-92-64-76737-9 (print)
ISBN 978-92-64-54785-8 (pdf)

OECD Studies on Water
ISSN 2224-5073 (print)
ISSN 2224-5081 (online)

Photo credits: Cover © Anna Vaczi/Shutterstock.com

Corrigenda to OECD publications may be found on line at: *www.oecd.org/about/publishing/corrigenda.htm*.

Foreword

With over 2 billion people without access to safe drinking water, 4.5 billion people lacking access to safely managed sanitation, and growing pressures on the quantity and quality of water resources, water and sanitation has been prioritised by the international community as Sustainable Development Goal (SDG) 6. But, it cannot be separated from all aspects of development; whether we achieve SDG 6 will impact every other SDG. Water and sanitation services and water resources management are especially relevant for food security, healthy lives, clean energy, sustainable cities, marine and terrestrial biodiversity and ecosystems. According to the World Health Organisation and UNICEF, 620 million children do not have decent toilets at school and around 900 million lack clean water to wash their hands. This discourages students, particularly girls, from attending school and completing their education. Better water and sanitation in schools is a practical measure to promote the education of the next generation of thinkers and leaders, especially women and girls.

A strong economic case exists for both governments and private actors to invest in water-related investments through blended finance. The annual economic losses due to inadequate water supply and sanitation are estimated at USD 260 billion. Projections of global financing needs for water infrastructure range from USD 6.7 trillion by 2030 to USD 22.6 trillion by 2050.

Although official development finance continues to be indispensable, these flows are far from sufficient to meet massive financing needs. Not only is there a need to unlock alternative sources of financing, but existing sources of finance can be deployed more strategically, so as to strengthen, over time, the financing systems required to deliver water and sanitation services and manage water resources sustainably. Blended finance, the strategic use of development finance for the mobilisation of additional finance towards sustainable development in developing countries, has a key role to play. Blended finance has the potential to attract additional commercial finance as well as act as a market building instrument to provide a bridge from reliance on concessional financing towards more self-sustaining financing approaches. The OECD's Development Assistance Committee (DAC) endorsed Blended Finance Principles in October 2017 providing guidance to donors in designing approaches that mobilise and better target commercial capital towards the full range of SDGs.

Taking stock today, we note that despite progress, blended finance has not gained sufficient traction for water-related investments. To encourage further action, this publication provides insights into how development actors can better deploy scarce financial resources and de-risking instruments to incentivise commercial actors to invest in water-related investments in developing countries. It assesses the instruments, actors and lessons learned from existing blended finance models for a diverse range of water-related investments. It identifies a variety of financial models that demonstrate how strategically deployed development finance can unlock commercial finance for these investments. The report also explores the potential for scaling existing approaches and for deploying blended finance for subsectors (such as off-grid sanitation), where commercial finance has yet to emerge. We would like to encourage stakeholders from governments, financial institutions and donors to draw on these lessons to explore how these models can be applied to new contexts. Our hope is that this work provides a foundation on which others can extend, adapt and scale up these models effectively.

This publication links to and complements two priorities of the OECD. First, the OECD's work on financing water including the Roundtable on Financing Water - a joint initiative of the OECD, the World Water Council, the Government of the Netherlands and the World Bank. Previous discussions at the Roundtable have helped to inform and shape this work and the platform provides an effective vehicle to disseminate the lessons learned. Second, on blended finance, we are working to develop the evidence-base and engage in co-ordination to ensure blended finance delivers on its potential. Under the Tri Hita Karana Roadmap for Blended Finance, a multi-stakeholder framework and partnership for mobilising commercial finance towards the SDGs, governments, development financiers and private sector entities are now working to make blended finance work at scale to deliver the SDGs.

This publication brings together the expertise and experience of these two communities and efforts to disseminate the key lessons from this report will continue to strengthen the linkages between the water and sanitation community and the blended finance community in order to deliver on the 2030 Agenda.

Rodolfo Lacy

Director of the Environment Directorate

Jorge Moreira da Silva

Director of the Development Co-operation Directorate

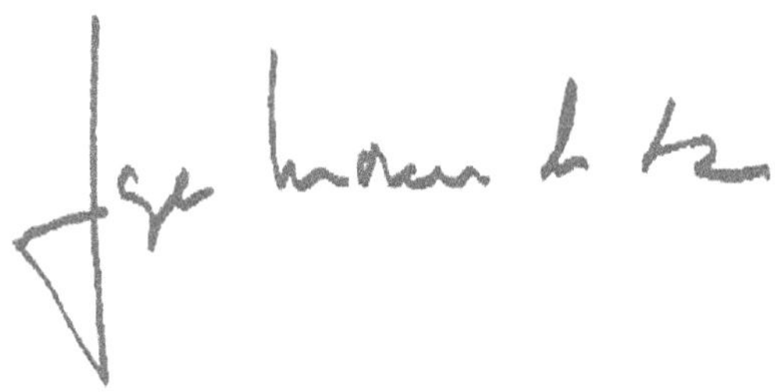

Acknowledgements

This report was jointly prepared by the OECD Environment Directorate (ENV), under the leadership of Rodolfo Lacy, Director, and the Development Co-operation Directorate (DCD), headed by Director Jorge Moreira da Silva. Kathleen Dominique (ENV) and Wiebke Bartz-Zuccala (DCD) managed and led the work to develop this publication. The core team responsible for drafting the publication included: Wiebke Bartz-Zuccala, Kathleen Dominique, Patrick Dougherty (DCD) and Chloé Desjonquères (ENV). Patrick Dougherty took the lead in researching, undertaking interviews, and drafting chapters 3 and 4 and the respective case studies. Chloé Desjonquères took the lead in researching, undertaking interviews and drafting chapter 2 and the respective case studies. Valuable inputs to earlier phases of the work were contributed by OECD colleagues, Tansher Singh and Carolyn Neunuebel. The work was undertaken under the supervision of Simon Buckle, Head of the Climate, Biodiversity and Water Division and Xavier Leflaive, Principal Administrator (ENV) as well as Haje Schütte, Senior Counsellor and Head of Financing for Sustainable Development Division and Paul Horrocks, Head of Private Finance for Sustainable Development Unit (DCD).

The OECD is grateful to the support, expertise and insights provided by Swedish International Development Co-operation Agency (Sida) and in particular, Karin Lindblad, Programme Manager. The authoring team is also grateful to all those who contributed expert insights, case studies and examples in the course of developing this work, including: Clément Frenoux and Olivier Crespi Reghizzi (Agence française de développement), Alyse Schrecongost (Bill and Melinda Gates Foundation), Amal Benaissa (BMCE Bank of Africa), Shubhagato Dasgupta and Ambarish Karunanithi (CPR India), Dinesh Mehta and Meera Meta (CEPT University), Konstant Bruinette (Development Bank of South Africa), Emilio Cattaneo (The Emerging Africa Infrastructure Fund), Thomas van Gilst and Patricia Castellarnau (European Investment Bank), Fabiana Velasques de Paula Machado and Raul Muniz Castillo Larissa Denea (Inter-American Development Bank), Matsumoto Shigeyuki (Japan International Cooperation Agency) Kumar Ranganthan and Gail Chambers (Millenium Challenge Corporation), Sophie Trémolet (The Nature Conservancy), Reint-Jan Deblois (VEI) and Antoon Blokland (BBO), Lesley Pories (Water.org), Dean Muruven (WWF), and Ziyanda Mpakama and Elizabeth Yaari (Stockholm International Water Institute). The team would also like to thank Souraya Chenguelly (The Stone Family Foundation), Dominique Carrie (Social Finance), and Pritha Hariram and Neinke Uil (FMO) for interviews and insights that helped shape the work.

The report also benefitted immensely from comments provided by delegates from the OECD Working Party on Biodiversity, Water and Ecosystems (WPBWE), external experts and OECD colleagues, including: Simon Buckle, Juan Casado-Asensio, Paul Horrocks, Xavier Leflaive, Alexandre Martoussevitch, Nestor Pelechà Aigües and Haje Shütte (OECD Secretariat), Clément Frenoux and Olivier Crespi Reghizzi (AfD), Alyse Schrecongost (Bill and Melinda Gates Foundation), Konstant Bruinette (DBSA), Fabiana Velasques de Paula Machado, Raul Munoz Castillo, Javier Garcia Merino, Yvon Mellinger and Sergio Campos (IADB), Mark Barnett (National Water Commission, Jamaica), Regina Rossmann (GIZ) and Shigeyuki Matsumoto and Chan Flerida (JICA), Brad Johnson (Resource Mobilisation Advisors), Lesley Pories (Water.org), Ella Lazarte (USAID).

The authors would also like to thank those that participated in the written consultation and provided feedback on preliminary findings in the course of the early stages of the project, including: Alex Money (Smith School, Oxford University), Monica Altamirano (Deltares), Arthur Wood (Total Impact Advisors), Karin Lindblad (Sida), Lesley Pories, Vedika Bhandarkar and Rich Thorsten (Water.org), Anton Earle (Stockholm International Water Institute) and Francois Brikke (Global Water Partnership).

In addition, the OECD would like to thank the organisations that supported or partnered with the OECD to convene various events that contributed to the development of this work, including: a dedicated session at the Stockholm World Water Week (August 2018), the OECD investor breakfast (September 2018), a joint conference with GIZ (October 2019), the 3rd meeting of the Roundtable on Financing Water (November 2018), the OECD/Sida hosted experts' meeting during the OECD Private Finance for Sustainable Development Week (January 2019), a dedicated session in the margins of the World Bank/IMF Spring Meetings (April 2019), and the 4th meeting of the Roundtable for Financing Water (June 2019).

A special thanks to the communications team for their dedicated support on the publication and related outreach, in particular, Sama Al Taher Cucci (ENV). The authors also extend their gratitude to Ines Reale (ENV) for excellent administrative support.

Table of contents

Tables

Annex Tables

Figures

Annex Figures

Boxes

Abbreviations and Acronyms

AAAA Addis Ababa Action Agenda

ACG Arab Co-ordination Group

ADB Asian Development Bank

AFD Agence française de développement

AfDB African Development Bank

ARIZ AFD's partial risk-sharing guarantee

BMGF Bill & Melinda Gates Foundation

BMZ Federal Ministry for Economic Cooperation and Development (Germany)

CAPEX Capital expenditure

CBS Container based sanitation

CEPT Centre for Environmental Planning and Technology

CPR Centre for Policy Research

CIV Collective investment vehicle

CrEW Caribbean Regional fund for Wastewater management

CRS Creditor reporting system

DAC Development Assistance Committee

DBOOT Design, build, own, operate and transfer

DBSA Development Bank of Southern Africa

DBP Development Bank of the Philippines

DFI Development finance institution

DFID Department for International Development (United Kingdom)

EAIF Emerging Africa Infrastructure Fund

EBRD European Bank for Reconstruction and Development

ECA Export Credit Agency

EDFI Association of European Development Finance Institutions

EGAT Electricity Generating Authority of Thailand

EIB European Investment Bank

EU European Union

EUR Euro

EWSA Energy Water and Sanitation Authority Rwanda

FAMM Monterrey Metropolitan Water Fund

FMO Netherlands Development Finance Company

FONAG Fondo Para La Protección Del Agua

FSM Faecal sludge management

FSTP Faecal sludge treatment plant

FTB Foreign Trade Bank

GEF Global Environment Facility

GIIN Global Impact Investing Network

GIZ Deutsche Gesellschaft für Internationale Zusammenarbeit

GUARDIAN Gramalaya Urban and Rural Development Initiatives and Network

HZL Hindustan Zinc Limited

IADB Inter-American Development Bank

IDA International Development Association

IFC International Finance Corporation

IIPSA Infrastructure Investment Programme of South Africa

IMF International Monetary Fund

IMP Impact Management Project

JCEF Jamaica Credit Enhancement Facility

JICA Japan International Cooperation Agency

JMD Jamaican dollar

KIS Kalangala Infrastructure Investment Services

KOMIDA Koperasi Mitra Dhuafa

KWL Kigali Water Limited

LBS Land-Based Sources

LDC Least developed country

LGUGC Local Government Unit Guarantee Corporation

MDB Multilateral development bank

MEWAR Managing Environment through Waste Reuse

MFI Microfinance institution

MIGA Multilateral Investment Guarantee Agency

MPWI Multi-purpose water infrastructure

MWI Ministry of Water and Irrigation in Jordan

NCB National Commercial Bank

NGO Non-governmental organisation

NRW Non-revenue water

NT2 Nam Theun 2

NTPC Nam Theun 2 Power Company

NWC National Water Commission, Jamaica

NZD New Zealand dollar

OBA Output based aid

ODA Official development assistance

OOF Other Official Flows

ODF Open Defecation Free

OECD Organisation for Economic Co-operation and Development

OPEX Operational expenditure

OPIC Overseas Private Investment Corporation

PDAM Perusahaan Daerah Air Minum

PDR Lao People's Democratic Republic

PhP Philippine peso

PIDG Private Infrastructure Development Group

PPA Power purchase agreement

PPIAF Public-Private Infrastructure Advisory Facility

PPP Public-private partnership

PWRF Philippines Water Revolving Fund

RCT Randomized controlled trial

RWF Rwandan francs

SAB Sustainability Awareness Bond

SDGs Sustainable Development Goals

SDIP Sustainable Development Investment Partnership

Sida Swedish International Development Cooperation Agency

SIWI Stockholm International Water Institute

SFF Stone Family Foundation

SPV Special purpose vehicle

TA Technical Assistance

TBC Toilet Board Coalition

TNC The Nature Conservancy

THK Tri Hita Karana Roadmap for Blended Finance

UN United Nations

UNCDF United Nations Capital Development Fund

UN DESA United Nations Department of Economic and Social Affairs

UNDP United Nations Development Programme

UNICEF United Nations Children's Fund

USAID United States Agency for International Development

USAID DCA USAID's Development Credit Authority

USD United States dollar

WASAC National water and sanitation utility

WASH Water, sanitation and hygiene

WCWDM Water conservation, water demand management

WHO World Health Organisation

WOP Water Operators Partnership

WSP Water Service Provider

WSPF Water and Sanitation Pooled Fund

WSS Water supply and sanitation

WWF The World Wide Fund for Nature

Executive Summary

Water-related investments are key for sustainable development and inclusive growth. Sustainable Development Goal (SDG) 6, the dedicated goal on the sustainable management of water and sanitation for all, has spill over effects across the SDG Agenda, including the goals on food security, healthy lives, energy, sustainable cities, sustainable consumption and production, and marine and terrestrial ecosystems.

Yet, according to WHO and UNICEF, as recently as 2015, 2.1 billion people lack access to safely managed drinking water services and 4.5 billion people lack access to sanitation compatible with the SDG 6 objectives (WHO/UNICEF, 2017[1]). Further, growing pressures on water resources degrade water quality and increase scarcity, as competition for the resource among various uses (cities, industries, farms and the environment) intensifies. The economic benefits of investing in water security could exceed hundreds of billions of dollars annually (Sadoff et al., 2015[2]). Yet, despite a strong economic case for such investment, financing persistently falls well short of needs.

Investments in water and sanitation services and water resources management have historically been financed by the public sector, with concessional finance playing an important role in developing countries. The mobilisation of private finance for the water sector has been limited to date. Risk-return considerations and structural issues related to profitability of operating business models often undermine commercial investment. While finance from domestic public budgets and development finance, particularly concessional finance, will continue to have an important role to play in the sector, these flows are not sufficient to address total financing needs.

Blended finance can play a critical role in mobilising commercial finance as well as strengthening the financing systems upon which water–related investments rely. The OECD defines blended finance as the strategic use of development finance for the mobilisation of additional finance towards sustainable development in developing countries (OECD, 2018[3]). Blended finance can add value by shifting funds that are currently not directed to sustainable development in countries and sectors that have significant investment needs in order to deliver on the SDGs.

The OECD, with the support of the Swedish International Development Agency (Sida), has undertaken research to better understand the current and potential role of blended finance models for water-related investments. Considering the wide variety of potential types of water-related investments, this research takes a broad approach to water-related investment and covers blended finance models that contribute to the SDGs including, but not limited to, SDG 6. Specifically, the report focuses on three subsectors: (1) water and sanitation utilities, (2) off-grid sanitation and (3) multi-purpose water infrastructure (MPWI), including emerging landscape-based approaches[1].

Based on findings from case studies, interviews, workshops and extensive desk research, this publication builds a robust evidence base on how blended finance can play a role in attracting commercial finance. It

[1] Landscape-based approaches consider the impacts of investments within a given spatial area (e.g. catchment or basin) and often integrate nature-based solutions.

provides examples of current good practices and trends, distil lessons learned and emerging guidance to scale such approaches in order to exploit the full potential of blended finance.

Blended finance models are emerging but have not reached scale. Blended financing models across the three subsectors reflect different stages of financial market building. Blended models to finance utilities have proven to be an appropriate tool for creditworthy or near creditworthy utilities to move away from purely concessional donor finance towards market financing. For off-grid sanitation, however, grants and concessional financing are predominant, whereas blended finance models that mobilise commercial financing are largely absent. In contrast, MPWI is a subsector where blended finance models are an established financing instrument mobilising commercial finance at scale. For landscape-based approaches, blended finance can potentially operate as a fit-for-purpose financing instrument as it brings together different stakeholders responding to their individual investment preferences, but developments in practice remain at a very early stage.

Effective blended finance instruments include guarantees and technical assistance. Guarantees, including credit risk and political risk guarantees, are an effective tool to mobilise commercial investment in the utilities and the MPWI subsectors. Development actors can use guarantees to limit the risk exposure and reduce the cost of capital from commercial lenders. Beyond guarantees, technical assistance at the transaction level plays a major role in water and sanitation. Technical assistance can have different entry points in blended finance transactions, including for project development, for investees such as utilities, or for financiers such as banks to set up new lending programmes tailored to the distinct needs of the sector. Technical assistance has a particularly crucial role to play in tailoring existing blended finance structures to local contexts.

The success of blended finance is dependent on the ability to mobilise domestic commercial investment tailored to the local context. Blended finance for water-related investments reinforces the need for, and benefits from, tailoring blended finance to the local context. In general, blended finance should aim to build local capital markets by working with and mobilising local financiers, as highlighted in the OECD DAC Blended Finance Principles. Water and sanitation services are, by definition, locally sourced and provided; water resources are best managed at the basin scale. At the same time, the sector requires strong public regulation due to the public good dimension of water and sanitation services and the common pool nature of water resources. These characteristics emphasise the need to work closely with local actors and align with local development needs.

There is a need to link blended finance approaches to the underlying value chain. To effectively tailor blended finance models for water-related investments, an understanding of the underlying business models and value chains is needed. Blended finance models can enter the sector at different points along the value chain, for example at the water provision or treatment level, downstream at the end-user level or at the investor level. Effective blended finance approaches take into account the underlying business models and respective revenue streams, and incorporate different stakeholder perspectives.

Pooling projects could be an effective way forward to address selected unfavourable project attributes. Providing commercial investors access to a variety of different transactions in the water and sanitation sector can mitigate concerns around small ticket size, risk exposure, limited sector or regional knowledge as well as high transaction costs. Pooling mechanisms such as blended finance funds tailor different risk and return profiles for individual investors, with development financiers often taking first loss and junior traches buffering the risk for commercial investors in the senior tranches. Guarantees, moreover, can strategically mitigate portfolio risk.

Design blended finance to build markets - and incorporate its subsequent exit. Blended finance is not about fixing issues in underlying business models. Beyond addressing a financing gap, it is a transitory market building tool that is designed to enable stand-alone commercial investment in the long-run, by providing confidence, capacities and track record in markets where commercial investors are not yet present. Blended finance, starting with concessional elements, should phase out over time and ultimately exit in order to prevent market distortion. An analysis of the exit strategy should be integrated in any programme design.

Beyond transaction-related insights into potential pathways to scale blended finance for water and sanitation, this publication derives policy level implications that aim to facilitate an uptake of blended solutions for sustainable development in the sector.

- **Design blended finance in conjunction with efforts to improve the enabling environment.** Blended finance cannot compensate for an unfavourable enabling environment, but rather needs to be accompanied by efforts to promote a stable and conducive policy environment. A weak enabling environment characterised by poorly designed or absent regulation, policies settings (e.g. water prices and tariffs), or institutional arrangements, compounded by political interference in the management of (often public) utilities, constrains commercial investment.
- **Increase transparency to make a valid business case for commercial investment.** Commercial investors are cautious about uncertainty regarding any of the risks related to an investment opportunity. With adequate contractual arrangement or blended instruments and mechanisms, it is possible to mitigate a variety of risks, share the remainder with the public sector or commercial co-investors, or take a certain level of risk on the financier's own book. However, in order to make such an assessment, risks associated with an investment should be transparent and quantifiable.
- **Establish policy-level co-ordination and co-operation processes for blended finance**. An excessive reliance on concessional finance can inadvertently crowd out commercial finance, creating market distortions that impede greater accountability and financial sustainability of the sector. Co-ordination and co-operation among development finance actors on their blended finance engagements is a key for the market building aspect of blended finance, particularly when a concessional element is involved. Development financiers should co-ordinate more structurally beyond single transactions. While there is general agreement about the need for improved co-operation, actions on the ground may remain fragmented.

1 Insights from blended finance in the water and sanitation sector

Scaling up investments in water and sanitation is a prerequisite to deliver the Sustainable Development Goals (SDGs), in particular SDG 6, which aims to ensure the availability and sustainable management of water and sanitation for all. Blended finance can be an effective tool to mobilise additional commercial finance and contribute to strengthening financing systems upon which sustainable service delivery and water resource management rely. This chapter provides insights into the state of blended finance for water-related investments drawing on analysis from three subsectors: (1) water and sanitation utilities; (2) small-scale off-grid sanitation services; and (3) multi-purpose water infrastructure and landscape-based approaches. The chapter documents insights drawn from experience with blended finance for water and sanitation to date and further explores the potential for scaling up.

1.1. Financing water to achieve the SDGs

1.1.1. Rationale

Water-related investments are key for sustainable development and inclusive growth. Sustainable Development Goal (SDG) 6, "ensure availability and sustainable management of water and sanitation for all" has spill over effects on a variety of further development challenges, including food security, healthy lives, energy, sustainable cities, sustainable consumption and production, and marine and terrestrial ecosystems (UN, 2015[1]). As of 2015, 2.1 billion people lack access to safely managed drinking water services and 4.5 billion people lack access to sanitation compatible with the SDG 6 objectives (WHO/UNICEF, 2017[2]). The economic benefits of investing in water security could exceed hundreds of billions of dollars annually (Sadoff et al., 2015[3]).

Projections of global financing needs for water infrastructure range from USD 6.7 trillion by 2030 to USD 22.6 trillion by 2050 (OECD, 2015[4]). In order to meet water, sanitation and hygiene (WASH) needs, USD 114 billion annual capital investment is needed to achieve SDG 6.1 and 6.2 alone by 2030, which can be up to three times the current level of investment (WHO/UNICEF, 2017[2]).

Water and sanitation has historically been financed by the public sector, with concessional finance playing an important role in developing countries. Official development finance1 contributes to financing water and sanitation in developing countries with USD 13.3 billion on average in 2016-17 (OECD, 2018[5]). While development finance, particularly concessional finance, continues to have an important role to play in the sector, these flows are not sufficient to address total financing needs and achieve the 2030 Agenda for Sustainable Development ("2030 Agenda"). Recently, the international development community has put the private sector at centre stage as a source for additional investments in sustainable development. However, private finance for the water sector has not reached the scale commensurate with the challenge2. Risk-return considerations and structural issues related to profitability of operating business models often undermine commercial investment.

Blended finance can be an effective instrument in mobilising commercial finance and strengthening the financing systems on which water-related investments rely.[3] Blended finance is the strategic use of development finance for the mobilisation of additional finance towards sustainable development in developing countries[4] (OECD, 2018[6]). By deploying development finance in a way that addresses investment barriers preventing commercial actors from providing capital in SDG-relevant sectors such as water and sanitation, blended finance operates as a market building instrument that provides a bridge from reliance on grant and other donor financing towards commercial finance. Development finance can include official and private finance, e.g. from foundations, with a development purpose. Commercial finance can include public finance, e.g. from sovereign wealth funds or public pension funds, and private finance, which is seeking market rate returns.

Blended finance can add value first and foremost by shifting funds that are currently not directed to sustainable development to countries and sectors that have significant investment needs in order to deliver on the SDGs. In doing so, blended finance enables commercial investors to develop a track record of operating in the sector by altering the risk-return balance in a way that the commercial sector is willing to invest. Due to their transitory nature, blended finance models should mobilise more commercial finance over time. In parallel, a larger role for commercial actors can enable stronger financial systems by encouraging accountability and transparency, as well as new ways of addressing existing social and environmental challenges. Social enterprises are, for instance, rethinking sanitation as a mode of service delivery rather than as conventional on-grid infrastructure.

Development finance actors, commercial investors and domestic actors, such as utility operators, have gained some experience with the use of blended finance approaches in the sector. However, thus far the role of blended finance in mobilising commercial finance for the sector is limited compared to other sectors.

Preliminary data on the amounts mobilised from the private sector by official development finance shows that USD 2.1 billion have been mobilised in the water and sanitation sector from 2012-17 (Figure 1.1) out of the total of USD 157.2 billion mobilised across sectors (OECD, n.d.[7]). This 1.36% share of private finance mobilised compared to the overall sample underlines the aforementioned challenges to mobilise private sector investment in the sector.[5] The banking and financial services, energy, industry, mining and construction sectors mobilised over 18 times the amount mobilised in the water and sanitation sector from 2012-17; mobilisation in agriculture was over twice as much.

In terms of blended finance instruments, guarantees mobilised 58% or USD 1.24 billion in the water and sanitation sector, followed by syndicated loans at 29% or approximately USD 0.6 billion. Comparatively, guarantees mobilised a smaller percentage of total private finance in all other sectors (40%), with direct investments representing a higher percentage of private finance mobilised in other sectors at 17% comparative to 7% of private finance mobilised in the water and sanitation sector.

Figure 1.1. Private finance mobilised by official development finance interventions by sector and instrument 2012-17

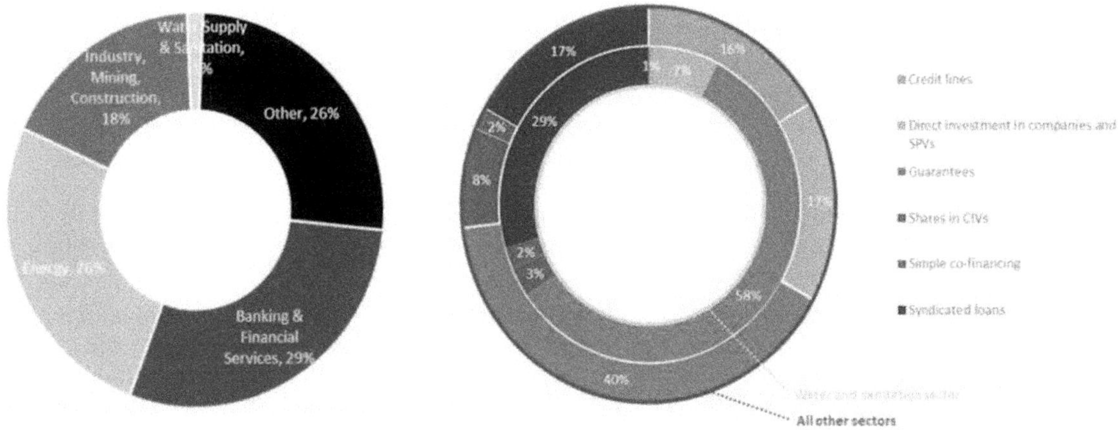

Source: (OECD, n.d.[7]), Statistics on amounts mobilised from the private sector by official development finance interventions as of July 2019, http://www.oecd.org/development/stats/mobilisation.htm

1.1.2. Approach and methods

A stronger evidence base is needed to better understand the current and potential role of commercial finance and specifically blended finance models for water-related investments. The relevance of the sector for multiple SDGs shows that water and sanitation investments can take a variety of forms and address a multitude of different needs. This publication therefore takes a broad approach to water-related investment and covers blended finance models that contribute to the achievement of the SDGs, including, but not limited to, SDG 6.

Analysis of blended finance in the water sector to date has focused mainly on water supply and sanitation services delivered by utilities.[6] This report builds on previous work to extend the analysis to examine the potential of blended finance for a broader range of water-related investments. As a basis for this research, a scoping study was developed to provide a typology of subsectors in the water and sanitation investment landscape to better understand the different risk and return characteristics and project attributes by subsector (OECD, 2018[8]). Based on a broad consultation process with donors, official development finance providers and commercial investors,[7] three fairly diverse subsectors were selected in order to provide distinct perspectives based on experience with blended finance to date, requirements for blended finance to successfully emerge, and potential for the use of different blended finance instruments and mechanisms. The selected subsectors[8] are:

1. Water and sanitation utilities: Water and sanitation utilities include public and private enterprises whose main purpose is the production, transmission, and distribution of water and sanitation services, including through water supply, wastewater collection and treatment, and the operation and maintenance of associated infrastructure (e.g. pumps, storage, pipelines, sewers etc.). The benefits of improved water and sanitation are social (e.g. improved human health and well-being), economic (e.g. improved productivity), and environmental (e.g. ecosystems and biodiversity) (OECD, 2011[9]).
2. Small-scale, off-grid sanitation: A range of technologies and service delivery models in this subsector can be used to deliver services for the safe disposal of human urine and faeces in settings where centralised, large-scale infrastructure is not cost-effective or is absent. Small-scale off-grid approaches are emerging in the absence of centralised sewerage systems particularly in large urban areas in developing countries, and are ideally complementary to the development of sewerage systems. In this subsector, innovative service delivery models have been developed and implemented by predominantly early stage enterprises.
3. Multi-purpose water infrastructure and landscape-based approaches: Multipurpose water infrastructure (MPWI) projects and landscape-based approaches (integrated projects within a given spatial area) deliver multiple water-related benefits across several sectors, for example to agriculture, energy production, fisheries, recreation and tourism. Projects incorporating landscape-based approaches are increasingly being developed to address SDG-related challenges.

Based on findings from case studies,[9] interviews, workshops and extensive desk research,[10] this publication seeks to build an understanding on how blended finance can play a role in attracting commercial finance to each of the subsectors, provide examples of current good practices and trends, and distil lessons learned and emerging guidance to scale and exploit the full potential of blended finance to deliver the SDGs.

The publication is structured as follows: Chapter 1 is a synthesis chapter of the lessons learned and insights from the analysis of the three subsectors. Chapters 2, 3 and 4 lay out the underlying detailed analysis for each subsector. This includes an introduction into each subsector, a commercial investor perspective on risk, revenues and project attributes, blended finance models and insights into the impact on sustainable development, as well as subsector specific insights.

1.2. The state of the blended finance market in water and sanitation

1.2.1. Blended finance models are emerging but have not reached scale

Blended finance models to mobilise additional commercial finance for water-related investments are emerging but have not reached scale. The analysis of water and sanitation utilities, off-grid sanitation, multipurpose water infrastructure and landscape-based approaches shows that this assessment varies by subsector given the heterogeneity of the operating models in each of them. In general, blended finance should aim to have a transitory nature over the long-run that works towards scaling the total financing available by crowding in the commercial finance at a transaction level. By doing so, it enables a capital market building process. Within this process, there are several stages, which characterise the interaction of development and commercial finance. Over time, there should be a shift from purely concessional development finance, to blending concessional development finance with non-concessional development finance (e.g. the blending of a donor grant facility with a development finance from public and private actors), to crowding in commercial finance (Figure 1.2) (OECD, 2018[6]). For water and sanitation-related investments, the public sector will likely continue to play a significant role in financing due to the public good dimensions of the sector, in addition to the governments' role in infrastructure more broadly.[11] Shifting towards an increasing share of commercial finance in the sector can not only increase the total amount of financing available, but also strengthen the financing systems[12] on which these investments rely and put the sector on a more sustainable footing.

Within this spectrum of blended financing, the three subsectors are characterised by transactions that reflect different stages of financial market building. Blended models to finance utilities are emerging as an appropriate tool for creditworthy[13] or near creditworthy utilities to move away from purely concessional donor finance towards market financing. For the off-grid sanitation subsector and technologies, however, grants and concessional financing are predominant, whereas blended finance models that mobilise commercial financing are largely absent. In contrast, MPWI is a subsector where blended finance models are an established financing instrument mobilising commercial finance at scale. For landscape-based approaches, blended finance can potentially operate as a fit-for-purpose financing instrument as it brings together different stakeholders responding to their individual investment preferences, but developments remain at a very early stage.

Figure 1.2. Stylised representation of the current state of transaction level mobilisation and market evolution over time

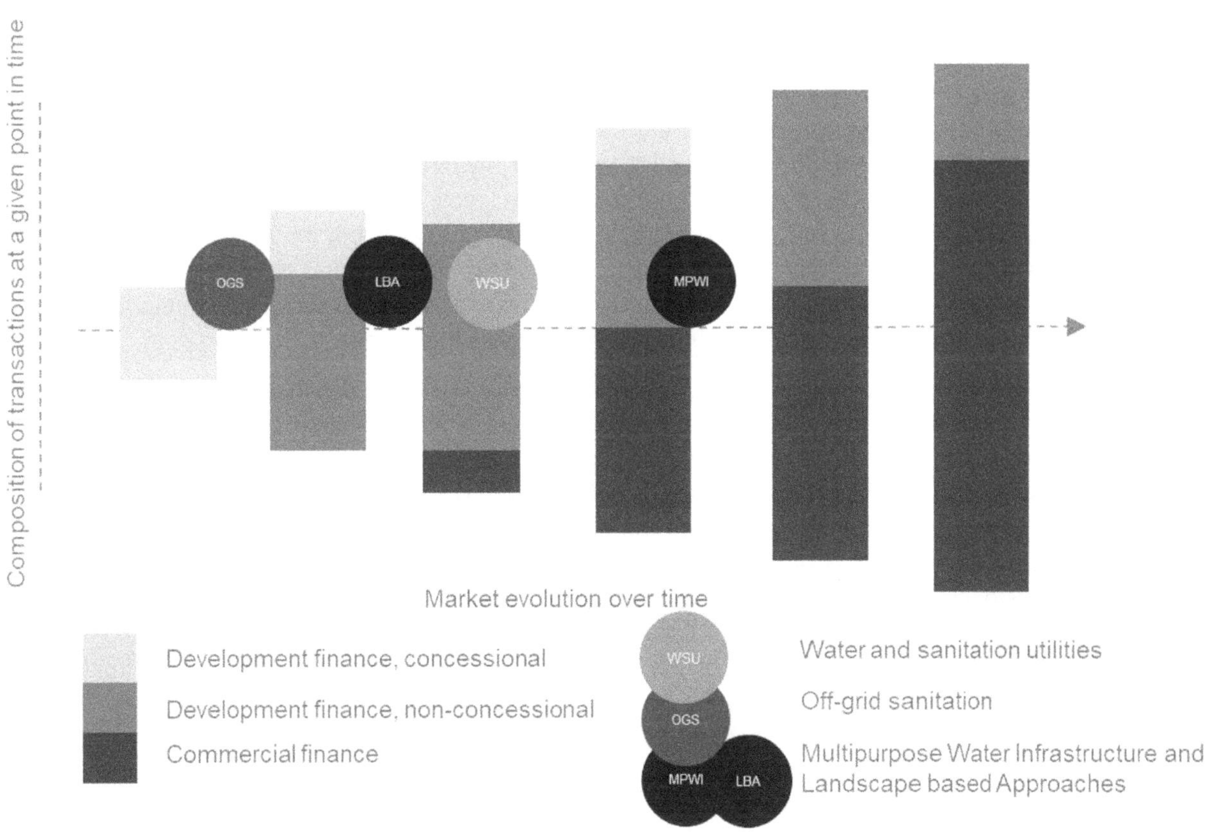

Source: Authors based on (OECD, 2018[6])

1.2.2. Specific investment attributes are limiting the engagement of commercial finance

In order to increase the mobilisation of commercial finance, the root causes of the current low level have to be assessed from a commercial perspective. A commercial financial actor such as a bank or asset manager defines an attractive investment opportunity by its project characteristics such as risk, returns and other attributes, including longevity or its potential to scale.[14] A variety of features undermines commercial investment at greater scale for water-related investments. These vary significantly by subsector, resulting in the need to identify tailored blended financing solutions by subsector and context linking particular investments and investor needs (Table 1.1).

A lack of sustainable revenue streams is holding back commercial investments

While the expansion of water and sanitation services is fundamental to achieve SDG 6, affordability constraints (perceived or real), particularly in lower income countries, often undercut a clear investment case. Revenues, however, are the main driver of financial sustainability and hence the potential return for commercial financiers and investors. Sustainable revenue generating business opportunities are in particular lacking for utilities and off-grid sanitation services.

Water utilities often fail to generate a sufficient revenue stream to cover operational and maintenance costs due to low rates of cost recovery and persistent operational inefficiencies. In addition, subsidies received by utilities typically benefit households that are already connected to the network, rather than those lacking access to services.[15] Pricing water and sanitation services generates revenues that can be used to maintain, renew and extend water infrastructure. If tariffs for water supply and sanitation (WSS) services are designed well, the revenues can be used to improve operational inefficiencies and to increase access to services among low-income households. In reality, however, many utilities do not fully recover operational and maintenance costs (OPEX),[16] let alone capital expenditure (CAPEX) via tariffs.

Affordability concerns (perceived or real) often lead political decision makers to keep tariffs artificially low, which contributes to the vicious cycle of decaying infrastructure and deteriorating services. Poor households are often willing and able to pay for WSS services, and water supply from a utility is often less costly than buying from private vendors. Despite willingness to pay by customers, political decision makers can be reluctant to allow utilities to raise tariffs to cost-reflective levels as they perceive this to be politically unpopular. Thus, a key barrier to expanding access to services is usually not the ability to pay for tariffs based on usage, but rather the ability to pay for connection fees (Leflaive and Horit, Forthcoming[10])(). Better targeting subsidies to extend the network to unserved customers or allowing customers to pay for connection fees over time, rather than in a lump sum can address this barrier.

In the off-grid sanitation subsector, currently, revenue streams are often insufficient to support private sector sanitation service provision. The current market structure is predominated by small, often nascent and financially unsustainable business models. Typically, social businesses provide off-grid sanitation services across the supply chain with a variety of different approaches resulting in a different revenue stream sources (see Figure 1.3). These include the sale of products like toilets, holding or septic tanks, vacuum trucks and faecal sludge treatment or reuse facilities, as well as revenue from products sold after processing of waste (compost, fertiliser etc.). Other revenue streams involve the provision of services and include user fees for toilets, the collection fees generated from off-grid waste treatment and waste treatment disposal or reuse. The pricing of the provision of off-grid sanitation services is limited by affordability. As a result, business models are not financially sustainable. For these businesses, break-even is often limited to OPEX. On the other hand, the complementary faecal sludge collection and treatment service ("waste-to-energy") constitutes a more profitable business opportunity that can become financially sustainable if a sufficient scale is reached, though this may be unachievable in smaller settlements where the number of end users is limited. In general, an observed pathway to sustainable revenues is to collaborate with local and national governments and water utilities. An example of this is the collaboration between Loowatt, a container based sanitation enterprise and the utility Laguna Water in Manila.[17] Loowatt successfully demonstrated its product and received a procurement request for toilets from the Laguna, thereby contributing to more stable and predictable revenues.

Figure 1.3. Potential revenues along the off-grid sanitation value chain

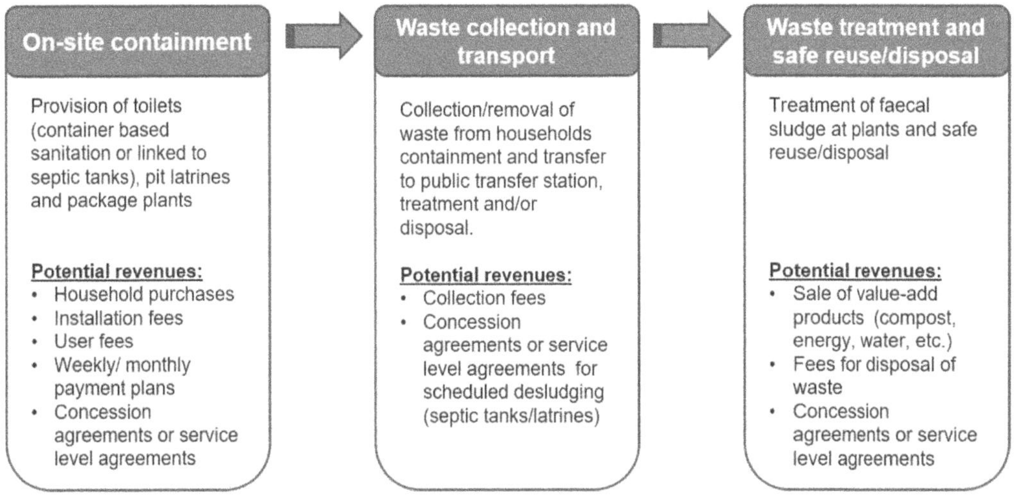

Source: Authors.

Blended finance models mobilise commercial investments in MPWI projects. As opposed to utilities and off-grid sanitation services, MPWI projects that include an energy element such as hydropower generate clear, stable and quantifiable revenue streams. This is for instance the case with tariffs and power purchase agreements (PPAs) for electricity produced or wastewater treated. The case of the expansion of the As-Samra Wastewater treatment plant in Jordan provides such an example. On the other hand, in some instances commercial investors may be reluctant to invest in multisector infrastructure as it is hard to value a project when the revenue is coming from different sources or diluted by business dimensions with less clear revenue generating opportunities.

Other project attributes are preventing commercial finance at scale

Beyond revenue-specific features that pose a challenge to commercial investment, attributes relating to risk and size include the attractiveness of water-related investments. For water and sanitation utilities, lack of creditworthiness constrains their ability to obtain commercial financing and they are often perceived as high-risk borrowers. In addition, commercial financiers have limited experience with and understanding of the sector. To palliate the risk of lending to utilities, commercial investors often offer shorter tenors (5 to 7 years) than the sector needs (at least 15 to 25 years),[18] together with high interest rates and collateral requirements.[19] Additionally, given the track record of heavy reliance on public and concessional finance, water service providers also often lack the skills necessary to support their funding applications with adequate documentation, including cost-benefit analyses and financial statements to demonstrate the level of profitability of the project. All of these elements limit utilities' ability to access commercial finance.

Off-grid sanitation businesses face challenges to generate demand for services, which is often also a reason for a lack of revenues at scale, in combination with affordability issues. For example, social enterprises providing container based sanitation (CBS) solutions in developing countries often face a dual challenge of creating the demand and building a market, and at the same time growing the business. As such, substantial resources need to be devoted to awareness raising and advocacy for this service. Public and development finance can also advance innovative faecal sludge management technologies to meet needs of communities unable to deploy conventional systems – such as in the case with Udaipur in India. The absence of a track record and knowledge base constitutes additional risks for the commercial investor. Finally, commercial investors are typically interested in large-scale investments in order to off-set transaction costs. Social sanitation entrepreneurs, however, have a limited capital absorption capacity and hence require investment at smaller scale.

In contrast, MPWI projects are typically large-scale projects that appeal to commercial investors. In addition, MPWI bring multiple actors together that contribute specific expertise in developing, financing, building and/or operating the infrastructure. In order to address the specific needs and roles, typically specialised enterprises are established (so-called Special Purpose Vehicles [SPVs]). SPVs constitute a well-known structure to commercial investors. At the same time, despite often predictable revenue streams, structural issues of large scale infrastructure projects are also prevalent in the MPWI space, including long and costly preparation, long-term financing tenors, as well as political risks which increases MPWI projects' vulnerability with respect to changing circumstances. For example, the large-scale Nam Theun 2 hydropower plant project and related environmental and social programme took over 30 years from inception to completion with numerous delays.

At the same time, a trend towards developing landscape-based approaches is emerging. MPWI projects are an established approach to deliver water-related services, typically with conventional "grey" infrastructure (conventional, built infrastructure). However, there has been an increased focus on the use of landscape-based approaches, which consider the impacts of investments within a given spatial area, e.g. catchment or basin, and often incorporate nature-based solutions. Increasingly, development actors are integrating landscape-based approaches such as integrated watershed management into their project development efforts. These efforts can provide opportunities for commercial participation, which previously did not exist. Stakeholders, such as water users (e.g. corporates with water-intensive activities in a basin) can be mobilised to finance such water-related projects. An example is Water Funds, collective investment vehicles, developed by The Nature Conservancy (TNC) and the Inter-American Development Bank's (IADB) Latin American Water Funds Partnership. Over 24 Water Funds have been set up in the region to date. The funds pool together grant funding from donors, water users, local communities and corporate entities within the spatial area or basin, to fund activities that improve water resources management, including reforestation, restoration and soil management to improve water infiltration. To date, however, these funds have not mobilised commercial finance.

Table 1.1. Summary of investment attributes across the three subsectors

Feature	Water and Sanitation Utilities	Off-grid sanitation	MPWI and Landscape-based Approaches
		Risk	
Macroeconomic and business risks	Currency risk (due to mismatch revenue and debt servicing currency), operating risk (weak performance of utilities), credit risk (inability of counterparty to honour contractual arrangements)	Currency risk (due to mismatch revenue and debt servicing currency), market risk (demand for service), operating risk (weak performance of sanitation service providers), liquidity risk (inability to exit/sell)	Currency risk (due to mismatch revenue and debt servicing currency), credit/off-taker risk (if applicable), operating risk (due to a variety of different technologies in MPWI), termination risk (risk of early termination of long-term contracts), market risk (demand for service), construction risk (if applicable)
Regulatory and political risks	Regulatory and political risk (sensitivities around water and sanitation tariffs and potential for political interference in the tariff setting process); economic regulation may be weak or absent (further, regulatory regimes may preclude the possibility of including debt service in the costs that can be covered by the tariff)	Regulatory risk (e.g. in many developing country contexts there is no regulatory environment for off-grid sanitation, political risk (in the case of government procurement contracts) and utilities may not have mandate to engage in non-sewered sanitation)	Regulatory risk (e.g. change in tariffs if any; private participation in infrastructure)

Feature	Water and Sanitation Utilities	Off-grid sanitation	MPWI and Landscape-based Approaches
Technical risks	Due to the long-lived and capital-intensive nature of water and sanitation infrastructure as well as under-investment in maintenance, performance risks may arise due to aging infrastructures, leakage and obsolesce of technologies. As water distribution infrastructure is underground and services can continue despite high levels of leakage, such degradation can go undetected for years, as rehabilitation and maintenance needs climb significantly.	Performance risk and obsolesce of utilised technology as off-grid sanitation approaches are as container based solutions (CBS) and faecal sludge management (FSM) technologies are relatively new	Obsolesce of utilised technology given the long-term nature of contracts and multitude of technologies applied.
Environmental/ social risk	Environmental risk (e.g. increasing water scarcity can lead to increase of cost of bulk water supply as a result from variability of rainfall and increasing uncertainty about future conditions). Social risks (e.g. particularly for low-income households, relative to tariff increases as a result of major new capital investments)	Environmental risk (e.g. chances of spillages of excreta of CBS and onsite sanitation)	Environmental risk (e.g. complex and costly assessment of MPWIs adherence to environmental standards; variability of availability of water resources due to climate change can reduce performance of MPWI, for example hydropower production). Potential negative environmental impacts of large MPWI, disrupting natural flow regimes that support ecosystem services. Social risk (e.g. the resettlement of households that will be flooded down stream of dams).
		Return	
Cash-flow generation	Utilities collect tariffs and other payments (e.g. connection fees) from customers. Tariffs can, but in practice often do not, fully cover operational and maintenance costs and rarely cover capital expenditure. Improvements in operational efficiency can create more cash flow to invest in service expansion and increase the customer base and revenues.	Depending on off-grid sanitation model, cash flows are generated through the sale of toilets (usually paid monthly), collection fees for waste, from products sold after processing of waste, user fees for toilets and concession contracts from local governments	MPWI projects often have quite predictable revenue streams, for example in case of electricity generation tariffs or power purchase agreements (PPAs) and large scale waste treatment plants. Cash-flows generated by landscape approaches to delivering water-related services often generate cash flows within actors operating in the spatial area, including by increasing turnover, efficiencies or reducing cost and expenditures of e.g. bulk water supply.

Feature	Water and Sanitation Utilities	Off-grid sanitation	MPWI and Landscape-based Approaches
Developmental return	Improved access to water and sanitation services produce a range of valuable benefits for individuals, communities and the environment, including a reduction in adverse health outcomes, increased educational attainment (especially for girls) and enhanced labour productivity.	Can reduce levels of open defecation and improve hygiene of households leading to reduced illness. Sanitation services also improve menstrual hygiene management (which, in turn, can reduce drop-out rates of girls in school). Properly managed waste reduces the environmental impact of poorly managed sanitation.	Projects can have potentially significant economic effect on areas. Landscape-based approaches can improved water management and quality for downstream users
		Project Attributes	
Greenfield vs. brownfield	Greenfield projects face additional business or technical risk due to the construction.	Not applicable given the service nature of the subsector.	Greenfield projects face additional business or technical risk due to the construction.
Scalability	Some projects and financing structures could be scaled and replicated, with adaptation to local contexts and institutional structures. Other models present limitations to replication due to specific contextual circumstances.	Off-grid sanitation models can be scaled in particular if they are seen complementary to sewered systems and as such can access a stable revenue source, e.g. a public off-taker. Any replication of project hence depends on the underlying jurisdiction and context.	MPWI and landscape-based approaches are significantly dependent on the spatial area where they are located, including the actors located in the areas. At the same time, in particular landscape-based approaches such as Water Funds have proven to be scalable and replicable when adapted to the local context.
Size	Depends on whether the water provider serves an urban or rural area. The population density of service area is a critical factor.	Small scale direct investment in enterprises.	MPWI are typically large scale projects run as Special Purpose Vehicles (SPVs). Landscape infrastructure projects tend to be smaller focusing on spatial area.
Transaction costs	High given weak capacity of service providers to maintain an asset registry and sufficient financial and accounting record keeping.	High given the opacity of small business typically low level of expertise in financing this sector.	Adapting projects to the local context comes with high project development cost.
Tenor/ Longevity	Minimum average of 15 years of debt financing for a sustainable debt service.	Varies, with the need for long term patient capital to develop and scale business models.	Long tenor of in particular MPWI public private partnerships (PPPs), e.g. 20-25 years.

Source: Authors.

1.2.3. A variety of blended finance instruments and mechanisms are already applied

Despite barriers related to the risk-return profile and project attributes of water-related investments, a variety of blended finance instruments and mechanisms are already being applied in the sector. For water and sanitation utilities, blended finance takes multiple forms in a variety of contexts. The research conducted for this report reveals varied blending experiences with different instruments (credit lines, guarantees, grants, etc.) and contexts (urban and rural; large and smaller operators). They also reveal that blending can happen at multiple entry points in the financing chain, such as upstream at the level of the lender or utility (technical assistance, loans, credit lines, guarantees), or downstream to customers (utility-based pro-poor financing schemes; access to microfinance loans). Critically, blended finance is often accompanied by technical assistance at all stages of the project.

For off-grid sanitation, grant funding appears to be the major source of finance. Philanthropic actors as the Bill & Melinda Gates Foundation (BMGF) or the Stone Family Foundation (SFF) contribute significantly in providing grant funding.[20] In addition, development agencies such as USAID or the Swiss SDC provide grant funding for backing innovative business models in the sanitation sector. A few social impact investors provide patient capital in this sector such as FINCA Ventures and Acumen, in addition to development finance institutions. At the same time, the bulk of grant funding appears to go to a handful of well-known social enterprises. The good practice examples of innovative business models examined in this publication have often received grant funding from multiple international actors. Blended finance models to unlock commercial investment for off-grid sanitation have not yet emerged, and commercial finance from banks or investments from asset managers is largely absent from the subsector at present. An exception is the financing further downstream to customers, where microfinance plays a role in financing access to sanitation assets.

For MPWI, blended finance models are an established financing instrument for typically large scale special purpose companies directed to delivering multiple water-related benefits. Development actors engage in providing equity and debt to such companies, underwrite guarantees to mitigate risk for commercial investors, provide viability gap grant funding, or engage in project development with the ambition to mobilise commercial financing. A range of commercial actors such as Standard Chartered, BNP Paribas and ING, for example, are involved in financing the Nam Theun 2 power plant. For landscape-based approaches, blended finance can potentially operate as a fit-for-purpose financing instrument as it brings together different stakeholders responding to their individual investment preferences. Technical assistance and pooling mechanisms are prevalent blending instruments; models that mobilise commercial financing are at a very early stage.

In terms of instruments, the use of guarantees is particularly effective in mobilising commercial finance across sectors through the mitigation of financial risk resulting in lower cost of capital. As noted above, guarantees account for 41% of private finance mobilised across all sectors (Figure 1.2), which holds for the water and sanitation sector, where guarantees are also the dominant instrument with 59% of private finance mobilised. This is mirrored in the case studies included in this publication.

Guarantees are most commonly used in blended financing for water and sanitation utilities. One example is the Philippine Water Revolving Fund (PWRF), which was set up with both primary and secondary guarantees provided a combination of public and private actors. The Local Government Unit Guarantee Corporation, a private entity, provided banks with a credit risk guarantee, which is backed by a co-guarantee from the USAID-Development Credit Authority (DCA). Additionally, JICA's concessional loan to the Development Bank of the Philippines is backed by a sovereign guarantee from the Government of the Philippines Department of Finance. Guarantees have also played an important role in MPWI projects. For example, GuarantCo provides a joint partial credit risk guarantee with USAID's DCA of USD 1.8 million to Nedbank as part of the financing for the Kalangala Infrastructure project, covering the non-payment of debt service. In addition, MIGA provided USD 91 million in political risk insurance for Nam Theun 2 Power Project (MIGA, 2006[11]).

Beyond guarantees, technical assistance (TA), provided in-kind or through grants, is an integral component of blended finance arrangements across the three subsectors. Technical assistance can boost investor confidence at the capital provider level or at the investee level. It is also critical at the project development stage (see Figure 1.4 for an overview of technical assistance models for water-related investments[21]). Technical assistance is therefore an effective tool to improve the investment-readiness of water and sanitation utilities by tackling both financier and investees confidence and shortcomings and is also applied in the MPWI sector to develop large-scale projects.[22]

Figure 1.4. Technical assistance models for water and sanitation

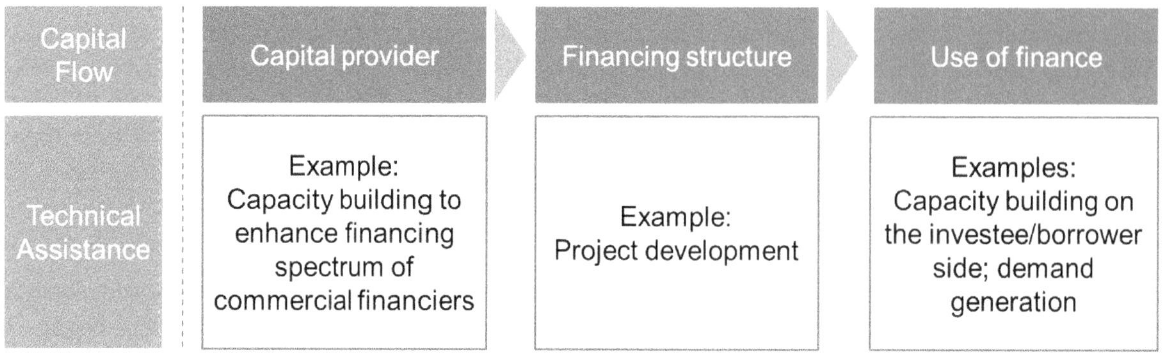

Source: Authors.

Capacity building can enhance the creditworthiness of utilities by improving their technical and financial performance.[23] Improvements in the quality of the service provided by the utility, such as achieving water supply continuity and improved water quality standards, can lead to demand generation, improved willingness to pay from customers due to service improvements and a larger paying customer base. This, in turn, leads to increases in revenues that, if well managed, contribute to the financial sustainability of the utility. The implementation of financing schemes adapted to the needs of the poor can further enlarge the utility's customer base.

Capacity building can also change the behaviour of commercial financiers and facilitate access to commercial finance for utilities. Water and sanitation utilities have specific needs when it comes to accessing finance, in part because they require long tenors in order to service debt while maintaining affordability. In addition, they often do not have sufficient levels of operational efficiency to guarantee rapid returns on the investment. Technical assistance can play a role in helping commercial financiers adjust their lending practices by creating financial products specifically targeting the needs of the sector, including longer tenors with an adequate grace period, and reduced collateral requirements. In Cambodia, the AFD-led project was instrumental in halving collateral requirements and doubling tenors from 5 to 10 years inclusive of a 12 months grace period. In doing so, commercial financiers diversify their portfolios of projects, thus reducing the risk of their overall investment portfolio risk.

TA is crucial to develop and fund large-scale MPWI projects that can attract commercial finance, particularly in the project development phase. For example, the Private Infrastructure Development Group's (PIDG) Technical Assistance Facility supported the development of the Kalangala Infrastructure Services (KIS) projects, a project that updated the water and transport infrastructure of Kalangala and which mobilised over USD 6 million commercial finance from the Nedbank Group. In addition, technical assistance from The Nature Conservancy (TNC) and the IADB has played a critical role in the creation and project investments of Water Funds, which are landscape-based approaches to mobilise local actors to finance watershed improvements across Latin America. Grant funding is also used for project development in the off-grid sanitation sector. Innovative financing models such as development impact bonds are increasingly explored to attract additional finance, for instance by Social Finance UK for the scaling up of faecal sludge management (FSM) services.

1.3. The potential of blended finance for water-related investments

1.3.1. Addressing operational bottlenecks can spur the uptake of blended finance instruments and mechanisms

Harness the opportunity to mobilise local commercial actors

Blended finance for water-related investments reinforces the need for, and benefits from, tailoring blended finance to the local context. In general, blended finance should aim to build local capital markets by working with and mobilising local financiers, as highlighted in the OECD DAC Blended Finance Principles.[24] Simultaneously, this approach addresses issues related to currency mismatches, when debt and revenues are generated in different currencies. Water and sanitation services and water resources are, by definition, locally sourced and provided.[25] These characteristics emphasise the need to work closely with local actors and align with local development needs. The local grounding of blended finance models spurs the opportunity to mobilise local actors.

Leveraging local commercial stakeholders with a stake in improved water resources management (e.g. agricultural producers, food and beverage companies, mining companies and other water-intensive industries) can be effective in financing landscape-based approaches. Landscape-based approaches to finance water resources management integrate and leverage the local perspective by definition. Local actors benefit from improved quality and reliability of water resources upon which local commercial players rely and these actors are well positioned to participate in financing infrastructure projects that integrate landscape-based approaches. Improved water resources management, better sanitation services or cheaper electricity could benefit those corporates operating in the area. For example, food and beverage companies, breweries or utilities operating within the river basin and relying on water resources may not have to finance their own water treatment plants if the quality of the resources improves. Hence, it is possible to demonstrate the business case for and direct financial impact of improving water resources management. This is also reflected in the observation that, in current financing models, grants are often sourced from commercial actors who are water users in the basin. Heineken, for example, invests in the Monterrey Metropolitan Water Fund (FAMM) in Mexico, where it operates a brewery.

Understand business models and revenue streams across the supply chain and develop matching blended finance approaches

The water and sanitation service value chain offers a variety of entry points where revenues can be generated and which can be targeted by blended financing approaches (see Figure 1.4).

In the off-grid sanitation subsector, the provision of sanitation services in developing countries is crucial for sustainable development but financially unattractive at this stage due to unstable and limited revenue generating capacity. The complementary "treatment" business, including faecal sludge collection and treatment service ("waste-to-energy") constitutes a more profitable business opportunity if a minimum scale is reached. However, the two services are often valued separately, even if not delivered from two different enterprises and therefore it may be appropriate to combine them. For example, the enterprise Sanergy operates across the supply chain, but with two distinct entities for each market segment; e.g. it provides sanitation services with its non-profit arm as well as faecal sludge treatment services as a for-profit business. Currently, philanthropic actors provide grant funding to the not-for-profit sanitation business pillar (usually the provision of toilets), and development finance institutions (DFIs) provide loans to the faecal sludge treatment and processing business. While the sale of reuse may still not cover a substantial portion of the operating sanitation budget (World Bank, 2019[12]), blended concessional finance models may play a role in scaling integrated business models that link the provision of sanitation to the treatment dimension by valuing them across the supply chain. Blended financing models could bring the two sides together by working towards scale by leveraging clearer revenue proposals to attract commercial finance, while using concessional development finance to back the underlying sanitation business. The concessional element may work towards building the market and to help enterprises achieve scale and ultimately attract commercial finance. That is, government or philanthropic grant facilities could be blended with development or commercial actors' resources to generate investment opportunities in the long run.

Landscape-based approaches can capture additional revenues and returns across the value chain to raise further types of financing. That is, successful landscape-based blended finance approaches can unlock commercial investment by applying an integrated approach across the value chain of water-related investments. Explicitly valuing the benefits of water-related investments and related beneficiaries can create more opportunities to profitable investments by monetising often implicit returns in addition to more explicit returns.

Explicit gains can occur directly in the project company/investee but also indirectly, within actors operating in the spatial areas e.g. a higher turnover or lower expenditures because of better watershed management in the area. These explicit returns can be accompanied by more implicit benefits, e.g. land and other asset appreciation for actors operating in the spatial area. By strategically linking these returns to an investment, local actors may be mobilised into providing capital in improvements in water resources management that spur such operational benefits. An example is the Water Funds endowment model, where commercial actors provide non-repayable capital and do not get any return on investment. Potential reflows and returns are reinvested in watershed management activities that benefit downstream water users. The profitability of such capital provision does not necessarily emerge from the revenues generated and profit accrued by the project itself, but by its impact on actors in the spatial area reliant on water resources. Development finance remains crucial in setting up such complex structures that take into account the needs of different commercial actors as well as the different sources and expectations regarding returns (see Figure 1.5).

Figure 1.5. An investor perspective on return sources in landscape-based approaches

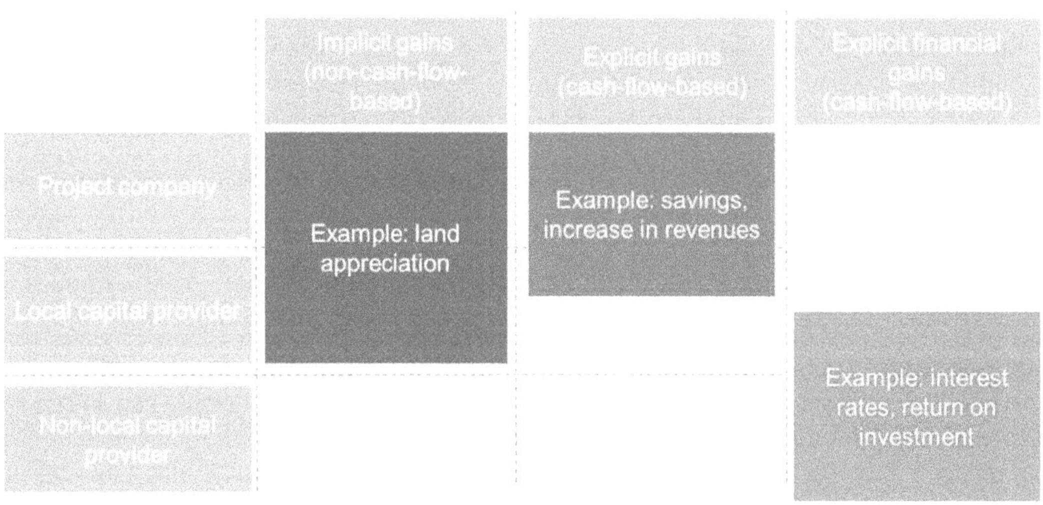

Source: Authors.

While models that mobilise funding from local stakeholders have emerged, stronger efforts are needed to better understand how commercial finance from local as well as non-local financial actors can be raised for such projects. For instance, financial institutions, local or international, are not accruing any implicit benefits of improved water-related services in the spatial area. However, external financing would be needed to scale and replicate successful models. That is, they need to realise explicit financial returns, for instance in the form of interest rates, which can put an additional burden on the project or company. Guarantees on debt service coverage or partial credit risk coverage by official actors could, for instance, play a role in mobilising commercial lending from local and international financial actors to project companies realising projects that result in water-related benefits, which in turn can strengthen their balance sheets.

Alternatively, equity instruments can be a successful instrument to mobilise commercial investment for landscape-based approaches. By definition, loans are fixed income instruments meaning that the interest rate does not mirror the underlying performance of the investee but is set *ex ante*. Consequently, the investor's participation in the performance of the investee is limited, which at the same time holds for the investor's exposure to losses. Implicit returns such as land appreciation, however, are not reflected in the return on debt financing. Blended models that introduce a shareholding perspective to the provision of financing can make a profitable business opportunity. In New Zealand, the Waikato River Authority introduced hybrid bond financing mechanisms that exhibit debt characteristics with a stable – and officially guaranteed - interest payment and at the same time equity characteristics by sharing the gains in land value with the investor. This OECD country example's replicability in developing countries has to be assessed. It spurs innovative thinking around overcoming the structural issues around landscape-based approaches.

Explore the development of a portfolio of projects to address selected unfavourable project attributes

Providing commercial investors access to a variety of different transactions in the water and sanitation sector can mitigate concerns around small ticket size, risk exposure, limited sector or regional knowledge as well as high transaction cost. Pooling mechanisms such as blended finance funds tailor different risk and return profiles for individual investors, with development financiers often taking first loss and junior traches buffering the risk for commercial investors in the senior tranches. Guarantees can moreover strategically mitigate portfolio risk. WaterEquity, for example, is a dedicated fund manager providing loans to a portfolio of microfinance institutions (MFIs) that on-lend microfinance loans for the purchase of water supply and sanitation assets. The set-up of a blended funds should be further explored in the sanitation space. Private equity fund models providing early stage, patient capital, or expansion financing could address a seemingly missing middle between grant funding and concessional debt financing. In financing landscape-based approaches, Water Funds are an established pooling model to mobilise grant funding from corporates. Finally, equity investing pooling mechanisms could be further explored to mobilise commercial investment into landscape-based approaches, which is currently absent.

Design blended finance to build markets - and incorporate its subsequent exit

Blended finance is not about fixing particular issues in underlying business models, nor is it only about filling a financing gap. It is a transitory market building tool that is designed to enable stand-alone commercial investment in the long-run, by providing confidence, capacities and track record in markets where commercial investors are not yet investing. Water and sanitation utilities that are moving towards creditworthiness can benefit from the elaboration of well-targeted blended financing strategies, for instance in support of improving their operational efficiency and financial sustainability. The experience of Water.org with Indonesia's Batang District utility suggests that not every water provider will be ready to immediately harness blended finance; a more phased approach may often be needed to ensure that the target institution is ready to manage commercial or blended solutions and their associated levels of complexity. In this context, the use of blended finance can facilitate market building because these utilities lack sufficient cost-recovery capacities to independently be financially sustainable, as well as the creditworthiness required to obtain commercial financing.[26]

At the same time, excessive reliance on concessional finance can inadvertently crowd out commercial finance. This can create market distortions that impede greater accountability and financial sustainability of the sector. For example, water and sanitation utilities with easy access to concessional finance have weak incentives to undertake the strengthening of their financial position required to access commercial finance.

The transitory nature of blended finance should be reflected in the phasing out of the concessional element, if any, followed by a phasing out of any development actor participation. A discussion on an exit strategy should be integrated in any programme design. For instance, in the case of Cambodia, AFD will soon initiate the phasing out of concessional finance from the Facilitating Access to Finance project as all funds available have been disbursed. Technical assistance has been key to risk reduction and to lowering borrowing costs for water service providers. Exit thus comes with specific challenges, to diffuse the technical assistance costs between the lender and the borrower without significantly raising the cost of the loan.

Co-ordinate stakeholders for the success of blended finance models

A lack of co-operation among the various stakeholders in blended finance transactions and programmes can constitute a barriers for the broader uptake of blended finance. Due to differing interests and mandates in blended arrangements, it is important that commercial actors, including private entities and private financing institutions, are involved from the project preparation phase of the project, together with all other stakeholders. This can ensure that all stakeholders have had a chance to participate in the negotiation regarding the options of viable instruments suitable to the different types of finance providers, that all agreements are concluded at the earliest stages, and that all information about the project is well communicated among all parties. Several blended finance arrangements suffer from significant delays at the onset of the project because of a lack of co-ordination and shared vision between stakeholders. The Jamaica Credit Enhancement Facility was delayed by two years because of lingering foreign exchange negotiations and procurement issues. The Kigali Bulk Water Supply also incurred delays due to disagreements over the currency of the loans as well as a late notice from regulators that they did not support the impact on water and sanitation tariffs. By contrast, in the case of the PWRF the effective donor co-ordination (between JICA and USAID) was instrumental in achieving complementary partnerships and defining innovative project concepts. Participating development agencies capitalised on their respective expertise and identified synergies to optimise the implementation of the project. This effective co-ordination built on a longstanding partnership between the two agencies, and was facilitated by frequent communications efforts. Co-ordination is thus essential to minimise delays in the implementation of the projects and ultimately avoid a rise in transaction costs.

1.3.2. Policy level considerations to make blended finance work for SDG 6

Design blended finance in conjunction with efforts to improve the enabling environment

Blended finance instruments and approaches cannot replace efforts to establish a robust policy and regulatory framework that water-related investments require. Due to the public good dimension of services provided and the monopolistic characteristics of service provision, the sector requires a strong regulatory and policy framework to function well. Moreover, water resources are a common pool resource, which requires robust allocation arrangements as well as policies and regulations to manage water quantity and quality (OECD, 2015[4]). A weak enabling environment characterised by poorly designed or absent regulation, policy settings (e.g. water prices and tariffs), and institutional arrangements constrains commercial investment (Pories, Fonseca and Delmon, 2019[13]). Blended finance cannot compensate for an unfavourable enabling environment, but rather needs to be accompanied by efforts to promote a stable and conducive policy environment.

For utilities, providing the financing needed to upgrade and expand their services is necessary, but it is not sufficient to make a blended finance arrangement work. Improving the enabling environment is equally important. Supportive policy reforms can increase water service providers' credit worthiness. For example, the government of the Philippines implemented policy reforms in the water and sanitation sector, including Republic Act 9275 in support of the implementation of the Clean Water Act and Executive Order 279, which shifts financing of creditworthy utilities to market and cost-based lending from banks. These regulations were instrumental in transferring utilities' demand for financing away from public sources. This not only avoided the crowding out effect, but also encouraged commercial financiers to extend their portfolio, diversifying their risk profiles and strengthening their capacity. While the PWRF stimulated private sector lending, continuing this innovative financing scheme depends on efficient implementation of policy reforms and market conditions.[27] Likewise, Jamaica's existing water and wastewater tariffs and the creation of the K-Factor system are evidence of the government's commitment to supporting the expansion and upgrading of its wastewater sector and of efficient communication and cooperation between government agencies, the National Water Commission, and the National Environment and Planning Agency. The Jamaican government also showed a strong will to reduce environmental degradation from untreated effluents through the 2013 wastewater and sludge reform, the 2015 ratification of the Cartagena Convention and associated technical agreement, and the alignment between its ambitions and the Caribbean Regional fund for Wastewater management (CReW) fund mandate. Under the second phase of the project, *Reforms for Wastewater Management*, additional tools were developed to further assist the government in improving the supporting environment.

In order to scale water-related investments, policy-related bottlenecks have to be addressed. In the case of MPWI, the Millennium Challenge Cooperation (MCC) designs its compacts , for instance in the case of Jordan, in conjunction with the governments to make MPWI most beneficial for the population but also vis-à-vis private investors. In the sanitation sector, a conducive policy and regulatory framework in developing countries could help container based sanitation (CBS) providers in moves towards reaching scale and provide greater clarity for investors. For example, CBS sanitation company X-runner, which operates in Peru, is unable to sell the compost it produces after treating faecal sludge on the open market as the legal framework does not exist – there are currently not faecal sludge treatment facilities in Lima and Peruvian law does not cover the reuse of faecal sludge produce (World Bank, 2019[14]).

Increase transparency to make a valid business case for commercial investment

Commercial investors are cautious about uncertainty regarding any of the risks related to an investment opportunity. With adequate contractual arrangement or blended instruments and mechanisms, it is possible to mitigate a variety of risks, share the remainder with the public sector or commercial co-investors, or take a certain level of risk on the financier's own book. However, in order to make such an informed assessment, risks associated with an investment should be transparent and hence quantifiable. For example, social and environmental risk assessments are inevitable to better understand the potentially negative social and environmental impact of large-scale MPWI projects. At the same time, such assessments are rather costly and lengthy. Development actors could engage in bringing their expertise to the table in conducting and financing such assessments, e.g. as in the case of Nam Theun 2 where the World Bank played a key role in developing and monitoring the environmental and social programme alongside the provision of financing.

In general, there is a need for more rigorous measurement, monitoring and evaluation of the development impacts of blended finance investments beyond the measurement of financial performances in order to prevent "impact" washing (OECD, 2019[15]). The development impact of water and sanitation projects with their public good nature is often complex to assess, in particular in large-scale multi-purpose water infrastructure projects. There is not coherent and common approach to measure incremental, causal and attributed impacts of specific investments. As this is not only the case in the water and sanitation space, efforts are ongoing that aim to establish common impact measurement and management frameworks.[28]

Transparency comes into play also in the project-tendering phase, when development actors need to understand with whom to work on the commercial actor side and vice versa. It is important for the commercial actor to understand the variety of blended models available.

Establish policy-level co-ordination and co-operation processes for blended finance

Co-ordination among development finance actors to co-operate on their blended finance engagements is a key success factor for the market building aspect of blended finance, in particular when a concessional element is involved. Development financiers should co-ordinate more structurally beyond single transactions. While there is general agreement about the need for improved co-operation, actions on the ground may remain fragmented. Blended finance should be part of the development of sector financing strategies and national investment plans related to SDG 6. Dedicated fora to discuss blended finance as an element of an explicit financing policy as well as issues around concessionality and crowding-in commercial finance are needed. Co-ordination on blended finance in water and sanitation will complement and link with several on-going international policy discussions related financing water. The Roundtable on Financing Water - a joint initiative of the OECD, the World Water Council, the Government of the Netherlands and the World Bank launched in 2017 - provides a global public-private platform with the aim to accelerate and scale up financing for water investments that contribute to sustainable growth. The Roundtable benefits from a strong engagement of several development finance institutions, a range of private financers and their institutional partners. Links to geographical efforts as the joint Arab Co-ordination Group (ACG) - OECD Development Assistance Committee (DAC) ACG-DAC Task Force on water and sanitation to achieve greater effectiveness and sustainable impacts in this sector should be explored.

Table 1.2. Blended finance for water and sanitation case studies undertaken

Case	Description	Country	Financing Sources	Financing Structure and Instruments used	Potential impact
			Water and sanitation utilities		
Kigali Bulk Water Supply	Construction of a water treatment plant.	Rwanda.	Private Infrastructure Development Group (PIDG): Technical Assistance Facility (TAF), Emerging Africa Infrastructure Fund (EAIF), DevCo; African Development Bank (AfDB).	Grants, Technical Assistance (TA), Debt, Equity.	Clean water supply to 500 000 inhabitants of Kigali.
Water.org	Scaling up microfinance loans in water and sanitation.	Indonesia, Philippines.	Water.org through philanthropic donations; local micro-finance institutions (MFIs).	TA.	Access to financing through WaterCredit loans for water and sanitation investments, Increased access to water and sanitation.
Jamaica Credit Enhancement Facility	Pilot of a credit enhancement facility.	Jamaica.	Global Environment Facility (GEF) Caribbean Regional fund for Wastewater management (CReW); K-Factor revenue reserve account.	Guarantee.	Pilot of a credit enhancement facility; Construction or rehabilitation of 8 wastewater treatment plants.

Case	Description	Country	Financing Sources	Financing Structure and Instruments used	Potential impact
Philippine Water Revolving Fund	Expand the loan portfolio of local banks to water and sanitation utilities.	Philippines.	Japan International Cooperation Agency (JICA), Development Bank of the Philippines, Private Finance Institutions, USAID-Development Credit Authority, Local Government Unit Guarantee Corporation.	Primary and Secondary Guarantees, Debt, Credit Line, Collective Investment Vehicle (CIV).	Expansion of utility services.
Access to Finance Project	Increase access to commercial finance of small-scale private water and electricity providers.	Cambodia.	Agence Française de Développement / French Development Agency (AFD), European Union, World Bank Water and Sanitation Program, Foreign Trade Bank (FTB).	Grants, TA, Credit Line, Guarantee.	Expansion and upgrading of rural utilities.
Blue Credit Line	Setting up of a credit line for water and sanitation projects	Morocco	European Investment Bank, AFD, BMCE Bank of Africa	Credit Line, TA	Increased operational efficiency of utilities
Water Operators Partnership	Cross-border technical assistance provision	Globally		TA	Increased operational efficiency of utilities
Cotonou Storm Water Management Project	Upgrading of the drainage, water and wastewater infrastructure in Cotonou	Benin	European Investment Bank	Debt	Reduced flood risk and impact on public health
Small-scale off-grid sanitation, wastewater collection and treatment					
Watercredit/WaterEquity	Scaling up microfinance water and sanitation loans.	Various		Debt	Increasing household access to water and sanitation.
Wai and Sinnar, two towns in India	Pilot of scheduled desludging and integrated waste treatment.	India	CEPT University, Bill & Melinda Gates Foundation, Municipal government and State Government of Masharawarta	Grant, TA	Demonstration of an approach for small and medium towns in India to achieve universal sanitation
Udaipur	Facilitating investments in waste treatment plants.	India	Bill & Melinda Gates Foundation, Centre for Policy Research India, Verdata	Grant, TA	Improving city level service coverage of safe waste disposal and reuse.
Multipurpose water infrastructure and landscape-based approaches					
Songwe River Basin	Development of integrated industrial irrigation, water supply, and hydropower projects.	Tanzania/Malawi	SIWI, Government of Tanzania, Government of Malawi, African Development Bank, private investors	Grants, TA, Debt	Enhanced food and energy security for the basin communities.
Nam Theun 2	Construction of a large scale hydropower plant as part of economic growth and poverty reduction plans.	Lao People's Democratic Republic	Government, World Bank, EIB, Thai Banks, Nam Theun 2 (SPV)	Debt, Equity, Guarantees	Funding for poverty reduction programmes from revenues and increased economic growth in the region.
MCC Jordan Compact	Expansion of As-Samra Waste Treatment plant and watershed management projects.	Jordan	Government of Jordan, MCC, Suez, Arab Bank	Grant, Debt, Equity	Increasing access to clean water and improving sludge management and

Case	Description	Country	Financing Sources	Financing Structure and Instruments used	Potential impact
					disposal processes.
Kalangala	Upgrading water/transport infrastructure and investment in renewables	Uganda	PIDG, local government, Nedbank	TA, Debt, Equity, Guarantee	Increasing access to safe water supply and access to basic infrastructure.
City of Tshwane	Large scale municipal water conservation, water demand management and cost recovery programmes	South Africa	DBSA, Infrastructure Investment Programme of South Africa, Private Investors	Grant, Debt	Reduced water losses in the distribution system, reduction in over consumption and improved billing and cost recovery rates
Latin America Water Fund Partnership	Pooled funding for effective watershed management across Latin America through landscape-based approaches.	Latin America	IADB, TNC, Global Environment Facility (GEF)	Grant, TA, CIV	Increasing water security for towns across Latin America.
Kafue River Basin	Funding water projects within Kafue River Basin including a wastewater treatment plant	Zambia	The World Wide Fund for Nature (WWF), Government of Zambia, FMO and private sector	Grant	Increasing food and water security for basin communities.

Source: Authors.

References

Andres et al (2019), *Doing More with Less: Smarter Subsidies for Water Supply and Sanitation*, World Bank, http://documents.worldbank.org/curated/en/330841560517317845/Doing-More-with-Less-Smarter-Subsidies-for-Water-Supply-and-Sanitation (accessed on 29 July 2019). [18]

Leflaive, X. and M. Horit (Forthcoming), *Addressing the social consequences of tariffs for water and sanitation*, OECD Publishing, Paris. [10]

Leigland, J., S. Trémolet and J. Ikeda (2016), *Achieving Universal Access to Water and Sanitation by 2030:The Role of Blended Finance*, http://documents.worldbank.org/curated/en/978521472029369304/pdf/Achieving-universal-access-to-water-and-sanitation-by-2030-the-role-of-blended-finance.pdf (accessed on 14 August 2019). [20]

MIGA (2006), *Hyrdopower in Asia: The Nam Theun 2 Project*, http://www.miga.org (accessed on 25 April 2019). [11]

OECD (2019), *Social Impact Investment 2019: The Impact Imperative for Sustainable Development*, OECD Publishing, Paris, https://dx.doi.org/10.1787/9789264311299-en. [15]

OECD (2018), "Blended Finance for Water Investment: Background Paper", OECD, Paris, http://www.oecd.org/water/Background-Paper-3rd-Roundtable-Financing-Water-Blended-Finance-for-water-related-investments.pdf (accessed on 25 April 2019). [8]

OECD (2018), *Creditor Reporting System (CRS)*, https://stats.oecd.org/Index.aspx?DataSetCode=crs1 (accessed on 3 January 2019). [5]

OECD (2018), *Making Blended Finance Work for the Sustainable Development Goals*, OECD Publishing, Paris, https://dx.doi.org/10.1787/9789264288768-en. [6]

OECD (2017), *OECD DAC Blended Finance Principles for Unlocking Commercial Finance for the Sustainable Development Goals*, https://www.oecd.org/dac/financing-sustainable-development/development-finance-topics/OECD-Blended-Finance-Principles.pdf (accessed on 6 August 2018). [16]

OECD (2015), *Water and Cities: Ensuring Sustainable Futures*, OECD Studies on Water, OECD Publishing, Paris, https://dx.doi.org/10.1787/9789264230149-en. [19]

OECD (2015), *Water Resources Allocation: Sharing Risks and Opportunities*, OECD Studies on Water, OECD Publishing, Paris, https://dx.doi.org/10.1787/9789264229631-en. [4]

OECD (2011), *Benefits of investing in water and sanitation : an OECD perspective.*, OECD. [9]

OECD (n.d.), *Statistics on amounts mobilised from the private sector by official development finance interventions as of 1st April 2019*, http://www.oecd.org/development/stats/mobilisation.htm. [7]

Pories, L., C. Fonseca and V. Delmon (2019), *Working Paper Mobilising finance for WASH: getting the foundation right*, https://www.ircwash.org/sites/default/files/mobilising_finance_for_wash_web.pdf (accessed on 31 July 2019). [13]

Sadoff, C. et al. (2015), *Securing Water, Sustaining Growth: Report of the GWP/OECD Task Force on Water Security and Sustainable Growth*, https://www.gwp.org/globalassets/global/about-gwp/publications/the-global-dialogue/securing-water-sustaining-growth.pdf (accessed on 1 July 2019). [3]

UN (2015), *The Critical Role of Water in Achieving the Sustainable Development Goals: Synthesis of Knowledge and Recommendations for Effective Framing, Monitoring, and Capacity Development*, https://sustainabledevelopment.un.org/content/documents/6185Role%20of%20Water%20in%20SD%20Draft%20Version%20February%202015.pdf (accessed on 12 July 2018). [1]

WHO/UNICEF (2019), *Data | JMP*, https://washdata.org/data (accessed on 8 July 2019). [17]

WHO/UNICEF (2017), *Progress on Drinking Water, Sanitation and Hygiene Update and SDG Baselines 2017*, https://www.who.int/mediacentre/news/releases/2017/launch-version-report-jmp-water-sanitation-hygiene.pdf (accessed on 14 August 2019). [2]

World Bank (2019), *Evaluating the Potential of Container-Based Sanitation: Sanergy in Nairobi, Kenya*, http://www.worldbank.org/gwsp (accessed on 23 April 2019). [12]

World Bank (2019), *Evaluating the Potential of Container-Based Sanitation: x-runner in Lima, Peru*, http://www.worldbank.org/gwsp (accessed on 6 May 2019). [14]

Notes

[1] This includes both Official Development Assistance (ODA), i.e. government aid with the main purpose of targeting economic development and the welfare of the developing country that are concessional in character, as well as other official flows (OOF), i.e. flows that do not meet ODA criteria, for instance in respect to concessionality.

[2] Further, in terms of distribution of blended finance across geographies, recent evidence shows that in the period 2012-17 only 6% (or USD 9.3 billion) of private finance was mobilised in Least Developed Countries (LDCs), whereas over 70% went to middle-income countries (OECD/UNCDF, 2019[8]).

[3] Blended finance is only one tool in development actor's toolbox and should be only applied when it leads to the maximum development outcomes, compared to other instruments available (see also (OECD[16])).

[4] See Annex A for further background on blended finance as well as blended finance instruments and mechanisms.

[5] No sector level data was available for the International Finance Corporation (IFC) for the year 2016-17.

[6] See, for example, (Leigland, Trémolet and Ikeda, 2016[20]), *Achieving Universal Access to Water and Sanitation by 2030: The Role of Blended Finance*, the World Bank Global Water Practice.

[7] Phase I of this research included extensive engagement and consultation at several events including: A presentation of a subsector scoping note at Stockholm World Water Week 2018, an OECD investor breakfast in September 2018, a joint conference with Deutsche Gesellschaft für Internationale Zusammenarbeit (GIZ) on behalf of the German Federal Ministry for Economic Cooperation and Development (BMZ) on "Closing the financing gap for water in line with SDG ambitions: The role of blended finance" from 4-5 October 2018, written consultation with key stakeholders on the subsectors of focus, and a presentation of preliminary findings and plans for Phase II at an OECD/Sida hosted experts' meeting as part of the OECD Private Finance for Sustainable Development Week.

[8] These subsectors are not mutually exclusive. Notably, water and sanitation utilities can play a role in delivery off-grid sanitation; multipurpose water infrastructure can include the delivery of water supply, sanitation and treatment services among other functions.

[9] An overview of case studies included in this publication can be found in Table 1.2.

[10] Phase II of the process and the analysis of this publication included requests for case studies of good practices from key stakeholders in the water and sanitation sector. Where possible these were followed up by interviews with experts and relevant officers, the OECD undertook phone interviews. The provisional findings of the report were presented at an OECD/Sida workshop for feedback and consultation as part of the Sustainable Development Investment Partnership (SDIP) Development Day at the side of the World Bank/International Monetary Fund (IMF) Spring meetings in April 2019.

[11] Blended finance in general is a tool in a toolbox including a whole variety of possibilities to fund projects. That is, public budget funding for instance remains an alternative, which blended finance does not aim to replace. Blended finance should be the financing tool of choice if it maximises development outcomes and impact, compared to other sources.

[12] This includes stronger accountability mechanisms between the lender, borrower and the beneficiaries of service delivery.

[13] Creditworthiness is not an abstract indicator that can be assessed in isolation of lending opportunities. In practice, it is measured against potential debt service payments from a commercial source and thus varies according to specific lending terms.

[14] These features are decisive in addition to investor individual preferences, as for example a geographical or sectoral focus.

[15] For further discussion, see: (Andres et al, 2019[18]) "Doing More with Less: Smarter Subsidies for Water Supply and Sanitation." Washington, DC; World Bank.

[16] Operational expenditure is accounting terminology and refers to business expenses that relate to operations, such as the cost of providing water supply, including salaries or energy. Capital expenditures (capex), on the contrary, refer to purchases of new assets, i.e. expansion or improvement of assets.

[17] Laguna Water is a piped water service provider jointly owned by the Provincial Government of Laguna (30%) and Manila Water Philippine Ventures (70%), owned by Manila Water Company a subsidiary of Ayala Corporation.

[18] Notably, many types of water infrastructure are very long-lived, with an economic life that can extend to 80-100 years or more, longer than most other public utility sectors (Hanemann, 2006).

[19] Collateral may include land titles or other forms of property provided by the borrower (rather than water infrastructure assets *per se*). See, for example, the case study on Cambodia.

[20] While philanthropic actors are very active in funding the sanitation sector, water and sanitation represents a minor share of overall philanthropic funds for sustainable development. OECD data shows that out of USD 6.1 billion provided for sustainable development by 26 foundations in 2017, USD 122 million are provided to water and sanitation, about 2%, see https://www.slideshare.net/OECDdev/private-philanthropy-for-development-2017-oecd-data.

[21] The OECD includes technical assistance in the set of blended finance instruments if related to a specific transaction or project (for more information, please see (OECD, 2018[6]).)

[22] Developing a continuous pipeline of projects remains challenging and requires close collaboration with governments, as well as subnational levels, given the cross-cutting nature of many MPWI projects.

[23] It is important to note that an effective regulatory environment, including cost-reflective tariffs, is a major component of the creditworthiness of utilities.

[24] (OECD, 2017[16]), OECD DAC Blended Finance Principles, https://www.oecd.org/dac/financing-sustainable-development/development-finance-topics/OECD-Blended-Finance-Principles.pdf

[25] At the same time, due to the public good dimension of water and sanitation services and the common pool nature of water resources, the sector requires a robust regulatory and policy framework to function well. However, in practice in many countries, that framework is weak or absent.

[26] In addition, credit ratings (or viable alternatives) can provide valuable information to potential lenders and investors regarding the creditworthiness of borrowers. For further discussion in the WASH context, see: (Pories, Fonseca and Delmon, 2019[13]).

[27] Building up on lessons learned from the PWRF, the Philippines has been implementing the Unified Financing Framework, its new financing policy with support from the World Bank and USAID. The new policy aims to: (i) align lending and financing policies to crowd in commercial financiers; (ii) rationalise government financing to non-creditworthy utilities; and (iii) establish an independent economic regulator and set pricing policy for wastewater management services.

[28] The OECD is a member of the Impact Management Project (IMP), a multi-stakeholder effort working towards a common framework. Moreover, under the Tri Hita Karana Roadmap (THK) for Blended Finance, which brings together blended finance stakeholders, a working group dedicated to the impact of blended finance is addressing that topic specifically for the blended finance space (see Annex A for further background on the THK Roadmap).

2 Evidence on blended finance in water and sanitation utilities

This chapter presents the results of the in-depth review of the water and sanitation utilities subsector, including (i) an introduction to the subsector, (ii) a commercial investor perspective, (iii) an overview of blended finance transactions, (iv) a typology of commercial investment ready to be mobilised, (v) an assessment of the impact on the poor, and (vi) subsector-specific lessons learned. Blended models to finance utilities are emerging as they are an appropriate tool for creditworthy or near creditworthy utilities to move away from purely concessional donor finance to more sustainable market financing.

2.1. An introduction to water and sanitation utilities

The water and sanitation sector encompasses water collection, treatment, and supply for domestic and industrial needs, and the operation of sewer systems and sewage treatment facilities that collect, treat, and dispose of wastewater. Water and sanitation utilities are entities that operate and maintain water supply and wastewater treatment facilities and infrastructure, thereby providing a service. These entities can be referred to as water and wastewater service providers.

Water and sanitation utilities are relatively heterogeneous depending on the specific context of service provision. Many developing countries present significant differences in the characteristics of utilities, particularly between urban and rural areas. Large-scale, centralised water and sanitation utilities tend to serve large urban areas, while small-scale, decentralised operators tend to be major service providers to low income households in urban and suburban areas, as well as to rural communities. Low-income households often make up the majority of under-served communities across both urban and rural areas. While utilities tend to be regulated, decentralised providers are largely informal and unregulated, and very often are the only available option to low-income households, for whom the connection cost of piped water and sewer can be prohibitive.

High rates of non-revenue water (NRW) are a notable problem in many developing (and developed) countries. NRW corresponds to the difference between the amount of water produced and supplied through the transmission and distribution network, and the actual amount of water billed to and paid for by customers. The two main sources of NRW are physical losses (real losses), due to leakage, and commercial losses (apparent losses), due to unauthorised consumption, faulty metering, or uncollected bills (Figure 2.1). As such, NRW is a major source of variable costs of a utility and an indication of the operational efficiency of the utility, the quality of the distribution network and commercial management practices.

Figure 2.1. Non-Revenue Water

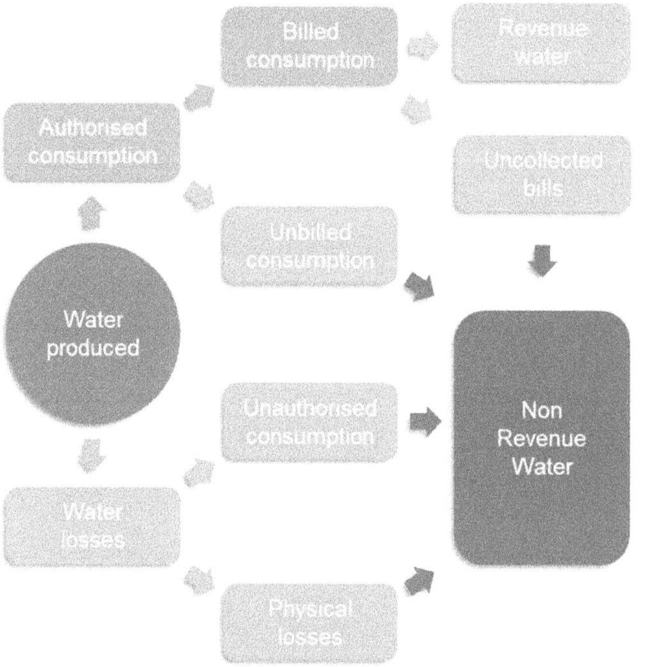

Source: Authors, based on (World Bank, 2006[1])

To limit NRW, utilities often resort to intermittent water supply and rationing. Providing uninterrupted water supply services prevents external infiltrations and the contamination of supplied water resources. However, the large leakages and deteriorating distribution networks can push utility operators to ration water supply to a few hours a day, which paradoxically contributes to a faster deterioration of the network infrastructure because of repeated water surges. This can lead to ruptured pipes and failing seals, ultimately increasing the operation and maintenance costs of the utility.

2.2. Investment profile: an assessment of the risks, returns and project attributes

Water and sanitation utilities are perceived by commercial investors as high risk investments due to inefficient operations, weak financial and management practices and limited cost recovery. As such they tend not to be financially sustainable enough to attract commercial financing. A summary of investment attributes is presented in Table 2.1 below.

Water and sanitation utilities' low creditworthiness undermines their ability to obtain commercial financing to maintain, expand and upgrade their infrastructure. Commercial financiers tend to be unwilling to lend to the water and sanitation sector because they may not be financially viable, although they are economically necessary, which is often the case with long-term, development-oriented infrastructure. As such, water and sanitation utilities are often seen as inefficient and unprofitable, thus high-risk investments. To palliate for that risk, banks often offer short tenors (5 to 7 years) than the sector needs (minimum of 15 to 25 years), together with high interest rates and collateral requirements. Additionally, water service providers also often lack the skills necessary to support their financing applications with adequate documentation, including cost-benefit analyses and financial statements to demonstrate the level of profitability of the project. All of these elements limit utilities' ability to access commercial finance.

Utilities in developing countries often operate in challenging environments. Water and sanitation operators not only face financial constraints, they also face weak enabling environments characterised by weak or absent policies, regulations and standards. Additionally, utilities often do not have sufficient technical expertise to best manage their operations and finances, and thus lack the capacity to comply with regulations and standards, when they exist. Utilities also often face political pressure to keep tariffs low, with detrimental effects on their cash flow generation. Fostering an enabling environment to support utilities' operations and improve the quality of service provided can be instrumental in the success of blended financing arrangements.

Table 2.1. Summary of investment attributes

Feature	Description
	Risk
Macroeconomic and business risks	Currency risk (due to mismatch revenue and debt servicing currency), operating risk (weak performance of utilities), credit risk (inability of counterparty to honour contractual arrangements)
Regulatory and political risks	Regulatory and political risk (sensitivities around water and sanitation tariffs and potential for political interference in the tariff setting process); economic regulation may be weak or absent (further, regulatory regimes may preclude the possibility of including debt service in the costs that can be covered by the tariff, thereby limiting the feasibility of access to commercial finance)
Technical risks	Due to the long-lived and capital-intensive nature of water and sanitation infrastructure as well as under-investment in maintenance, performance risks may arise due to aging infrastructures, leakage and obsolesce of technologies. As water distribution infrastructure is underground and services can continue despite high levels of leakage, such degradation can go undetected for years, as rehabilitation and maintenance needs climb significantly.
Environmental/ social risk	Environmental risk (e.g. increasing water scarcity can lead to increase of cost of bulk water supply as a result from variability of rainfall and increasing uncertainty about future conditions). Social risks (e.g. particularly for low-income households, relative to tariff increases as a result of major new capital investments)
	Return
Cash-flow generation	Utilities collect tariffs and other payments (e.g. connection fees) from customers. Tariffs may not fully cover operational and maintenance costs and rarely cover capital expenditure. Improvements in operational efficiency can create more cash flow to invest in service expansion and increase the customer base and revenues.
Developmental return	Improved access to water and sanitation services produce a range of valuable benefits for individuals, communities and the environment, including a reduction in adverse health outcomes, increased educational attainment (especially for girls) and enhanced labour productivity.
	Project attributes
Greenfield vs. brownfield	Greenfield projects face additional business or technical risk due to the construction.
Scalability	Some projects and financing structures could be scaled and replicated, with adaptation to local contexts and institutional structures. Other models present limitations to replication due to specific contextual circumstances.
Size	Depends on whether the water provider serves an urban or rural area. The population density of service area is a critical factor.
Transaction costs	High, given weak capacity of service providers to maintain an asset registry and sufficient financial and accounting record keeping.
Tenor/ Longevity	Minimum average of 15 years of debt financing for a sustainable debt service.

Source: Authors.

2.3. Blended finance instruments and mechanisms for financing water and sanitation utilities

Despite challenges to engage commercial finance noted above, the blended financing of water and sanitation utilities can take multiple forms in an array of contexts. The case studies, interviews and research conducted for this report revealed varied blending experiences with different instruments (credit lines, credit enhancements, grants, etc.) and contexts (urban and rural; large and smaller operators). The research also revealed that blending can happen at multiple entry points along the financing chain, such as upstream, at the level of the lender or utility (technical assistance, loans, credit lines, risk-reducing guarantees), or downstream to customers (utility-based pro-poor financing schemes, access to microfinance loans), and is often accompanied by technical assistance at all stages of the project.

Guarantees are the most commonly used credit enhancing tool in the blended financing of water and sanitation utilities. Guarantees can lower both the political and commercial risk of lending to utilities (OECD, 2018[2]). In a guaranteed arrangement, the guarantor agrees to their obligation to service the loan in the event that the borrower cannot repay. This obligation limits incurring losses for the commercial lenders, thereby increasing their willingness to finance a project. The Philippine Water Revolving Fund (PWRF) had primary and secondary guarantees in place: a credit risk guarantee provided participating banks with a partial guarantee from the Local Government Unit Guarantee Corporation (LGUGC) - a private entity - that covered a maximum of 85% of the bank's exposure against a 1% guarantee fee. This primary guarantee was backed (up to 50% of the LGUGC's exposure) by a co-guarantee from the USAID Development Credit Authority.

Credit enhancement can be a powerful tool to allow existing revenue streams to be used as collateral. In 2008, the Office of Utilities Regulation of Jamaica allowed for the tariffs of the National Water Commission (NWC, the water and sanitation utility of Jamaica) to include a "K-Factor", a pre-determined surcharge collected monthly from customers. The K-Factor revenues capitalise a special account earmarked for priority water and wastewater investment projects. Rather than using the K-factor revenue directly for capital investment, the accrued funds aim at servicing large commercial loans to finance investments in non-revenue water reductions, sewerage, and other operational efficiency processes. In the 2009-15 and 2016-18 periods, the K-Factor amounted to a 14% and 16% surcharge of the household bill.

Despite these efforts, the NWC continued to face difficulty in accessing the capital needed to expand and upgrade its water and wastewater services. The Global Environment Facility-funded Caribbean Regional Fund for Wastewater Management project (CReW), which aims at reducing the negative impacts of untreated wastewater on the environment and human health in the Wider Caribbean Region, selected Jamaica to pilot a credit enhancement facility. Credit enhancement improves the credit profile of structured financial products or transactions. The Jamaica Credit Enhancement Facility (JCEF) (Figure 2.2) placed a USD 3 million grant from the CReW in a reserve account as a guaranteed fund. With a 4:1 leverage of financial resources, the JCEF allowed for the fund capitalised by the CReW grant to provide secondary collateral against the USD 12 million loans disbursed by the National Commercial Bank (NCB) to the NWC. The debt servicing for the loan stems from annual K-Factor revenue. This instrument reduced the financial risk of the lender (NCB) and allowed greater access to commercial capital through the provision of a steady revenue stream earmarked for investments in priority wastewater and water supply projects.

Figure 2.2. The Jamaica Credit Enhancement Facility

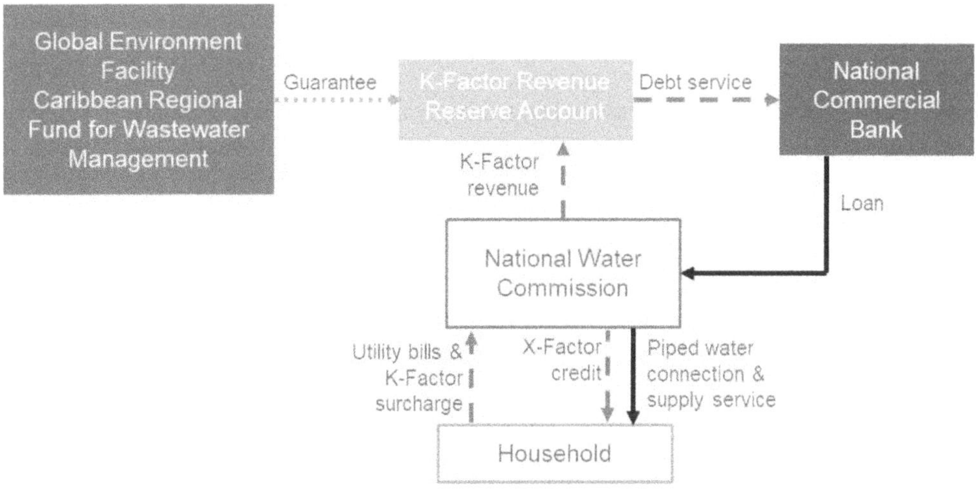

Source: Authors.

Another effective pooling mechanism in mobilising commercial finance is through *investment funds* or *collective investment vehicles* (CIVs). Funds pool resources to invest in specific sectors (or regions) using different type of instruments, including equity, debt or guarantees (OECD, 2018[2]). For instance, the USD 234 million Philippine Water Revolving fund (PWRF) (Figure 2.3) blends domestic public funds of the Development Bank of the Philippines (DBP) -which received a concessional loan from JICA-, with commercial financing from finance institutions at a 75%-25% ratio from each source respectively. This set up aims at sharing risk-return profiles, lower borrowing costs, and to market water and sanitation projects to private finance institutions. The PWRF revolves principal repayments on the loans while interest rates payments service blended contributions from the DBP and local banks. In order to mitigate the liquidity risks of the banks involved, the DBP uses the loan from JICA to create a credit line that the bank can rely on to disburse its share of the blended loans.

Figure 2.3. The Philippine Water Revolving Fund financing structure

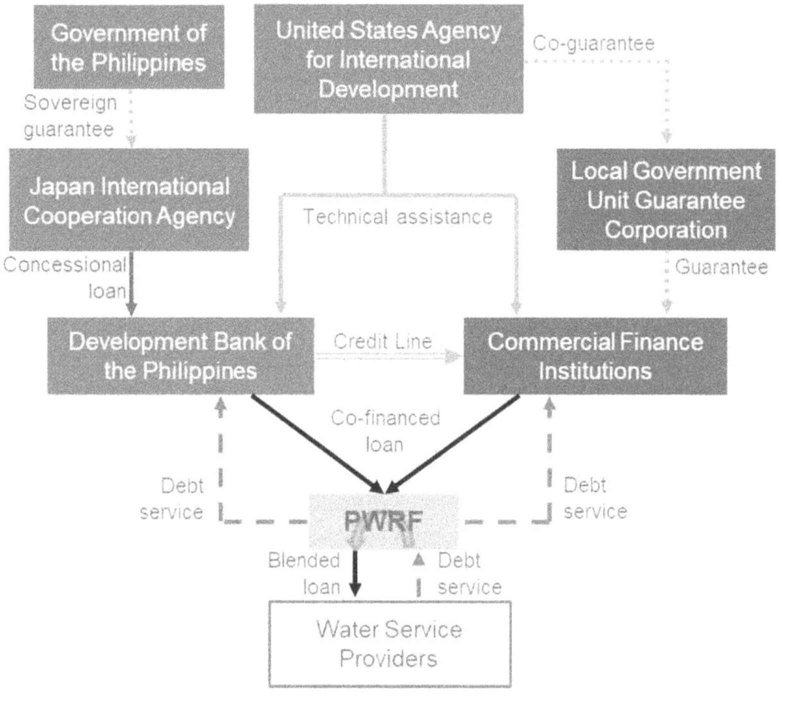

Source: Authors.

Credit lines are a conditional avenue to provide private financial institutions with capital to on-lend to water and sanitation projects. Furthermore, by providing utilities with access to dedicated commercial financing, the long-term aim is to enable them to build the capacity and creditworthiness they need to attract market-based financing. In Morocco, BMCE partnered with the French development bank (AFD) and European Investment Bank (EIB) to set up the Blue Credit Line, a facility to encourage investments in the water and sanitation sector and increase the climate resilience of the country (Box 2.1). This credit line provides earmarked funds for BMCE to offer below market rate loans to water and sanitation utilities, along with technical assistance to both the bank and the borrower. Similarly, a credit line accompanied by technical assistance was established on concessional terms in Cambodia between the AFD and the Foreign Trade Bank (FTB), with funds earmarked for loans in the water and electricity sectors. The concessional nature of that credit line ensures lower interest rates so that loans are affordable to small- and medium- sized utilities, and that tenors are long enough with a sufficient grace period. To securitise this credit line, AFD also set up a partial guarantee through its ARIZ scheme, which enabled FTB to share the portfolio credit risk with the AFD. The guarantee was instrumental in giving the FTB the confidence to lower collateral requirements by half compared to the initial obligation.

Box 2.1. AFD-EIB-BMCE Blue Credit Line

Protecting water resources for greater resilience to climate change

The preservation and protection of water resources is a key issue for Morocco. The country's high reliance on the agricultural sector and low economic diversification are strong elements of its vulnerability to climate change, with significant changes in precipitation and temperature projected for the region. Morocco has made notable progress in providing access to safely managed water supply, with an increase from 55% in 2000 to 69% in 2015 (WHO/UNICEF, 2019[3]). Nevertheless, Morocco is still facing drawbacks in the management of water resources, and because of population growth and economic development, water needs are increasing. The total volume of wastewater discharged by the industrial sector is estimated at 80 Mm3 per annum (the equivalent of 32 000 Olympic swimming pools). This is projected to increase as the country is pursuing an industrialisation strategy focusing on urban jobs creation, along with a focus on minimising environmental damage. Additionally, there remains around 8 000 polluting industrial sites in Morocco, and about 85% of these sites are located in urban areas served by a collective sewerage system. The overexploitation and inefficient use of the country's water resources, as well as lagging domestic and industrial wastewater treatment and, finally, ongoing climate change, are putting pressure on water resources. Some of these challenges can be attributed to a lack of investment in efficiency measures for water use and the treatment of polluted water. Obstacles to investment include limited financial access for project promoters; the fragmentation of small-scale investment opportunities; low cost of water resources for consumers; a lack of capacity to perform a cost-benefit analysis to evaluate an investment's profitability.

In this context, BMCE Bank of Africa partnered with AFD and the EIB to create the Blue Credit Line "*CAP BLEU*", a EUR 20 million financing facility dedicated to the implementation of projects in the water and sanitation sector in Morocco. This facility aims to respond directly to the sector's investments constraints through the provision of a dedicated credit line, with a reduced interest rate for project promoters, and concessional technical assistance to support both the bank in the assessment of the technical, financial and environmental feasibility of the projects and the structuration of such projects by the promoters. AFD and EIB, together with BMCE, developed the eligibility criteria for the Blue Line, which enabled the development of the offer. AFD finances the technical assistance "CEP - Marketing and Project Evaluation", aimed at accompanying and reinforcing BMCE capacities in the water sector, while the EIB finances the technical assistance "PP - Preparation of Projects" which aims at support companies (end customers) in the technical and financial preparation of credit applications to the Blue Facility. For sanitation and wastewater treatment projects, the technical assistance will certify that the investments financed will at least ensure compliance with the discharge standards in the environment or with the specifications for connection to the sewerage network, as well as ensuring water savings and reduced leaks. Targeted projects include treatment plants, desalination, water savings in irrigation, industrial depollution and reuse of treated water and recycling.

Source: Inputs shared by BMCE.

In the majority of cases, *technical assistance,* provided in kind or through grants, is an integral part of blended finance arrangements. Technical assistance can play a key role in boosting investor confidence at multiple levels (Figure 2.4).

Figure 2.4. Technical assistance models for water and sanitation

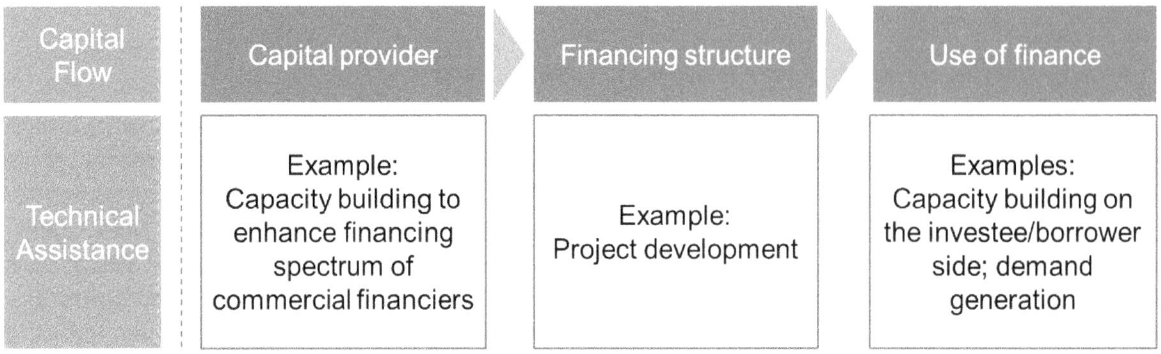

Source: Authors.

In the project preparation phase, technical assistance can support government institutions with policy advice. In Rwanda, technical assistance was instrumental in helping structure WASAC, the newly established national water and sanitation utility, to ensure it has the capacity needed to off-take the wastewater treatment plant from the Kigali Water Limited company when the Build-Operate-Transfer agreement expires. In Jamaica, the GEF's environmental focus contributed to ensuring that the credit enhancement facility fully integrated the reduction of pollution in water bodies in its strategy. The support of the government was a driver of the success in achieving high standards, as it not only ratified important treaties, but also passed key legislation and strengthened the capabilities of its institutions to enforce its water quality standards as a result.

Technical assistance can also support commercial financiers through capacity building, for instance in assessing the profitability of a project. As part of the BMCE Blue Credit Line, and AFD Facilitated Access to Finance for Domestic Private Water Operators in Cambodia, technical assistance provided to local banks increased their capacity to perform a cost-benefit analysis to evaluate an investment's profitability. The concessional nature of the technical assistance grant is critical in addressing the capacity gap of financial institutions in better assessing project proposals, and its cost will need to be shared between the borrower and lenders in the context of phasing out of the blended finance arrangement over time.

Technical assistance is often deployed to enhance utilities' creditworthiness through capacity building. Such assistance can be effective at reducing water losses, improving billing and collection rates, and improving the management of the utility. To address the issue of low operational efficiency, amongst others, Dutch utilities provide peer support to developing country utilities, an example of win-win cross-border co-operation detailed in Box 2.2 below. Strengthening the technical capacities of the operator contributes to improving the utilities technical performance, thereby enhancing their creditworthiness. Water service providers also often lack the skills necessary to support their funding applications with adequate documentation, including cost-benefit analyses and financial statements to demonstrate the level of profitability of the project. In Cambodia, development providers set up a technical assistance program to ensure that loans were disbursed to well-operated water service providers (WSPs). In doing so, the program provides WSPs with direct technical assistance in the management of their operations, from financial management to the control of the quality of the water supplied.

Technical assistance can also contribute to generating demand and increasing number of paying customers. In the Philippines, the Narra Water utility had received a concessionary loan to expand its infrastructure, for which it required revenue from a larger customer base to repay. Water.org provided them with concessional assistance in identifying those potential clients and marketing to them. Additionally, Water.org, through its WaterCredit initiative, encouraged local microfinance institutions (MFIs) to develop water and sanitation microloan products. These MFIs could then disburse WaterCredit loans to the new Narra Water clients who desired to connect (see section Chapter 3 for more information on WaterCredit and microfinance sanitation loans). Water.org also accompanies local utilities in improving their operational efficiency, and extending their infrastructure to poor communities to maximise their outreach and increase their paying customer base.

Beyond improvements in the operational and financial management of utilities, technical assistance and grants can support utilities in developing pro-poor pricing schemes. As part of the Facilitated Access to Finance project in Cambodia, development finance providers offered subsidies to reduce the cost of the connection for low-income households. In order to incentivise WSPs and ensure that low-income households had access to a continuous water supply with functioning metering, the WSPs received a pro-poor subsidy on an output-based basis, whereby they had to charge the lower fee to the household, and could only claim the subsidy once the connection had been established, and the metered connection verified. The implementation of financing schemes adapted to the needs of the poor can further enlarge the utility's customer base, in turn increasing its financial sustainability.

Box 2.2. Water Operators Partnerships

Implementing improved processes and pro-poor strategies through peer-support

Water Operators Partnerships (WOPs) are peer-support mechanisms designed to improve the operational efficiency and cost-recovery of water utilities in developing countries. Through the pairing of two or more 'mentor' utility companies in support of 'mentee' utility companies, hands on operator expertise and solutions are exchanged. WOPs aim at increasing the creditworthiness of the mentee on a not-for-profit basis. The objectives of these WOPs differ between projects, from the provision of technical assistance and training to the improvement of operations and maintenance for the reduction of non-revenue water, and developing infrastructure investment projects. According to the UN-Habitat's Global Water Operator Partnerships Alliance, the organisation leading behind WOPs, over 300 WOPs have been established globally since 2010.

WOPs have the potential to rapidly achieve capacity building and improved performance in developing countries. The VEI-Dawaco WOP (between the Da Nang Water Supply Joint Stock Company (Dawaco) in Da Nang, Vietnam, and Vitens Evides International (VEI), an organisation that manage the Water Operator Partnerships of five Dutch water utilities), aimed to enhance Dawaco's capacity and performance, and increase its creditworthiness through 3 objectives: i) the extension and improvement of water services in the city of Da Nang, Vietnam; ii) strengthening managerial and financial capabilities; and iii) extending services to the urban poor. The WOP also contributed to increasing VEI's experience in Corporate Social Responsibility projects.

The VEI-Dawaco WOP made significant progress on its objectives in less than 3 years. By 2010, the project had achieved non-revenue water reductions to 26% from 39% in 2007 (and further down to 15% by 2017) and an estimated 49 000 new water services connections, including 7 800 poor households. In terms of financial and operational management, the project contributed to the installation of water management systems to track water quality and quantity at water treatment plants as well as water resources; a new tariff structure was implemented in 2011 and incorporates a pro-poor strategy to make low-cost consumption accessible to households in need; and steps were taken to equitize Dawaco, which became a limited liability company in June 2010 (it previously was a state-owned enterprise), and a joint stock company in 2016. Overall, the total cost of the WOP was USD 2.7 million was financed by the Directorate-General for International Cooperation (DGIS) of the Netherland's Ministry of Foreign Affairs (USD 1.9 million), in-kind contributions from Dawaco (USD 282 500), and VEI (USD 550 000).

WaterWorx, a new partnership between Dutch Government and 10 Dutch Water Utilities, was launched in March 2017 with an aim to provide access to safe drinking-quality water to 10 million people worldwide by 2030. Through this programme, Dutch water supply companies will mentor 24 utilities across Africa, Asia, and Latin America in achieving infrastructure expansion and rehabilitation, and operational efficiency. The programme is supported by the Dutch government, with 55% of the first stage's EUR 54 million budget financed by the Dutch Ministry of Foreign Affairs, and the remaining 45% by participating Dutch and local water utilities. The Ministry also supports the initiative with technical assistance in policy, law and regulatory environments, in order to increase the credit-worthiness of participating utilities and foster long-term private investments in the sector. To meet the 2030 objective, it is estimated that EUR 1.5 billion of infrastructure investments are needed. Through WaterWorX, the Dutch water supply companies support their colleagues in identifying and prioritising investment projects, acquiring the needed investment finance to implement the infrastructure development projects and provide the needed capacity building for investment implementation.

Source: Authors, based on inputs from WOP.

2.4. A typology of investors in water and sanitation utilities

Development and commercial actors have different interests when financing projects. Commercial entities will evaluate an investment's profitability, while development institutions will take development outcomes into account in their decisions.

Commercial finance from local financial institutions is a primary source of the commercial financing raised through blended structures for water and sanitation utilities. Blended finance can target local banks in order to boost their confidence in lending to water and sanitation utilities. As explained above, finance institutions tend to be unwilling to lend to the water and sanitation sector because utilities may not be financially viable, although they are economically necessary, which is often the case with long-term, development-oriented infrastructure. Blended finance thus acts as a risk-reducing mechanism to increase banks' confidence and offer more suitable lending products, with reduced interest rates, longer tenors, and suitable grace periods and collateral requirements. At the same time, technical assistance as part of a blended finance package can support increased operational efficiency and financial sustainability in utilities. In Jamaica, the NWC had a ring-fenced fund in place, however given the very high rates of NRW, that fund by itself was not sufficient to unlock debt financing. In this context, Jamaica's JCEF provided a second guarantee to the fund that, together with the development of an ambitious infrastructure upgrading project, was eligible to serve as the main collateral for the loan.

Development actors as *Development Finance Institutions (DFIs) and Multilateral Development Banks (MDBs)* also play a major role in utility financing. This was the case in the Kigali Bulk Water Supply project. As part of the structuring of the financing, the Government of Rwanda agreed with development finance stakeholders - the IFC, three PIDG facilities, and AfDB - that the project would be a Public-Private Partnership (PPP) arranged on a Build – Operate – Transfer basis, the first of its kind in Sub-Saharan Africa (excluding South Africa). As the national water and sanitation utility (WASAC) had recently been established, it was not financially viable at that stage, thus a private utility was established as the Kigali Water Limited and handed over to Metito, who was awarded the bid order to implement the PPP and to build, operate, and maintain the treatment plant for 27 years before handing it over to WASAC. DFIs provided a majority of the financing through loans, grants and technical assistance, and the private utility provided the balance (18%) as equity financing.

Bi-lateral development banks and agencies, such as AFD, JICA, and USAID, contribute to mobilising private finance through a variety of instruments at different levels. Their participation can focus on building the capacity of banks and utilities through technical assistance and concessional debt, and on boosting investors' confidence with credit lines and guarantees. As part of the Facilitating Access to Finance project in Cambodia, AFD set-up a concessional credit line to cover the financial institution's liquidity risk, along with a partial guarantee to reduce its credit risk. AFD also co-ordinated an EU grant for technical assistance to build the capacity of the bank and of water operators to assess the feasibility and profitability of a project and ensure its quality. Development agencies may also contribute with concessional loans, and acting as co-guarantors, which were the respective roles of JICA and USAID's Development Credit Authority in the PWRF.

There is potential to mobilise *commercial investors* at scale**.** The EIB recently launched its Sustainability Awareness Bond (SAB), which it announced in April 2018. The new bond product aims at supporting the global goals by contributing to the development of a sustainable financial system through the financing of water and wastewater projects. In September 2018, the EIB issued its first EUR 500 million SAB. SAB eligibility is open to projects that contribute to the implementation of the SDGs without any geographical restriction. By December 2018, EUR 128 million has been allocated across 15 projects in 12 countries, including Senegal (28%), Italy (22%), Egypt (16%), and Panama (10%). Of these, 52% went to wastewater collection and treatment projects (EUR 65.6 million), 45% to water supply (EUR 55.8 million) and the remaining 3% to flood protection (EUR 3.6 million). SABs are a "use of proceeds" type of bond, meaning that disbursements for an SAB-eligible project will be funded from a dedicated account, where all funds raised through the issuance of SABs are managed by the EIB to finance solely water-related projects that meet the bond criteria. An example of an SAB-eligible project is outlined in Box 2.3 below.

Box 2.3. The EIB Sustainability Awareness Bond

Example of an eligible project

In Benin, the city of Cotonou, located below sea level on a coastal plain between the Atlantic Ocean and the Nokoué Lake, experiences cyclical floods during rainy seasons. Cotonou is the main economic centre of the country and hosts most of the economic and industrial infrastructure of the country. The floods cause large-scale damage to public and private assets and undermine economic activities. Additionally, Cotonou's rapid urbanisation rate is stressing the city's insufficient and poorly managed water and sanitation infrastructure. As a result, flooding frequently exposes the city's 1.5 million inhabitants to stagnant rainwater, resulting in adverse health outcomes, including typhoid fever and diarrheal diseases.

In December 2018, the government of Benin signed a EUR 50 million (USD 59 million) loan agreement with EIB for the financing of Cotonou's Storm-water Management and Urban Resilience Project. EIB's financing is part of a total cost estimated at EUR 128 million (USD 151 million), with additional financial support expected from the World Bank, AFD, the Islamic Development Bank, and the West African Development Bank. The programme consists in the construction of a storm-water retention pond, wastewater disposal infrastructures, and 47 roads to protect over 1.2 million people vulnerable to displacement, diseases, and material losses caused by the cyclical floods experienced every rainy season. The project aims at supporting sustainable growth and improving wellbeing, health and environmental outcomes by i) preventing flooding and the stagnation of rain water in the city, damage to urban dwellings and drainage infrastructure; ii) ensuring effective storm-water and wastewater drainage to improve sanitary conditions; iii) raising public awareness on hygiene, waste management, and sanitation; and iv) improving the quality of life of the inhabitants of several disadvantaged neighbourhoods through the provision of additional urban amenities (Republic of Benin, 2019[4]).

Although not explicitly stated in the loan agreement, the Cotonou project is 100% SAB eligible, providing an illustration of the types of projects that could qualify. The loan, which has been signed between the Finance ministry of Benin and the Bank is in line with EU legislation on water projects.

Source: Authors, based on inputs provided by EIB.

Non-governmental organisations (NGOs) may use donations to blend technical assistance and grants with commercial financing to increase access to water and sanitation. Water.org, through the provision of technical assistance and small grants to microfinance institutions (MFIs) fosters the creation of new loan products suited to the needs of water and sanitation projects and low income households. Its WaterCredit initiative (Figure 3.2 in Chapter 3) encourages the disbursement of microloans earmarked for water and sanitation projects by covering the costs of the project preparation phase, and assisting the MFI with the development of an adequate loan product and its marketing. By extending MFIs' portfolios with water and sanitation loans, Water.org also contributes to supporting SDG 8.10 "Strengthen the capacity of domestic financial institutions to encourage and expand access to banking, insurance and financial services for all". *NGOs* can also act as a stepping stone to unlock additional financing for utilities. Water.org also assists utilities with technical assistance in order to strengthen their operations, improve financial management, and increase their paying customer base. In Indonesia, Water.org's support to the PDAM utility was instrumental in unlocking over USD 51 000 in grant funding from the government to extend their pipeline to connect an additional 5 000 households.

2.5. An assessment of sustainable development impact

Inadequate access to safely managed water and sanitation can have numerous escalating impacts -- from the proliferation of infectious diseases and premature deaths to the contamination of clean water sources and the environment and the destruction of biodiversity.

Blended finance can have demonstrated impacts on commercial financiers, from the testing of new financing vehicles and the creation of tailored financial products for water and sanitation utilities, to the improvement in lending practices. In the Philippines, the PWRF successfully encouraged banks to offer water operators longer tenors (increased from 7 to between 15 and 20 years) at lower, fixed interest rates. Notably, in the cases studied, the blended finance arrangements were conducive to the development and diversification of local banks' portfolio of projects. The technical assistance they received enabled an increased understanding of the sector, and a better capacity to assess projects appraisals. In Cambodia, a technical assistance grant was disbursed to assist the FTB bank both in developing more adequate financial products for the sector, and in increasing its capacity to understand technicalities of water and sanitation to better assess project proposals.

Most cases studies examined in this report also demonstrated visible impacts on utilities through improvements in their operational efficiency and financial sustainability, which increased their creditworthiness. The resulting access to commercial finance also led to an increase in their paying customer base.

Overall, the blended financed projects studied have a considerable impact on development, not only by increasing access to water and sanitation in developing countries, as seen in Kigali, where the soon-to-be completed Bulk Water Supply project is expected to serve half a million people, but also to low income households, as in Cambodia, where 44% of the project's beneficiaries were poor households. Some projects also served as a means to increase access to finance, whether when unlocking a loan earmarked for the construction, decommissioning or rehabilitation of wastewater treatment plants in Jamaica, or through the introduction of WaterCredit, microfinance loans to finance poor households' water and sanitation projects.

2.6. Subsector-specific insights

- Water and sanitation utilities have distinct needs when it comes to accessing finance, in part because they require long tenors in order to service debt while maintaining affordability, and also because they often do not have sufficient levels of operational efficiency to guarantee attractive risk-adjusted returns on investment. Dedicated funds and facilities can tailor financing models to the specific needs of the sector. A recent development on this front is the Water Finance Facility, which seeks to mobilise large-scale private investment from domestic institutional investors (e.g. pension funds, insurance companies) by issuing local currency bonds in support of domestic priorities on water and sanitation. The first such facility is the Kenya Pooled Water Fund (KPWF), which has been initiated in Kenya with support of the Dutch government, Kenyan authorities and other development partners.
- Water and sanitation utilities that are moving towards creditworthiness can benefit from the elaboration of well-targeted blended financing strategies, for instance in support of improving their operational efficiency and financial sustainability. In this context the use of blended finance can serve the market building purpose, because these utilities lack sufficient cost-recovery capacities to independently be financially sustainable, as well as the creditworthiness required to obtain commercial financing.
- Capacity building as technical assistance is a common instrument in the blended financing of utilities. By improving the technical and financial performance of the utility, technical assistance

contributes to enhancing the creditworthiness of utilities. Improvements in the quality of the service provided by the utility, such as achieving water supply continuity and improved water quality standards, can lead to demand generation, improved willingness to pay from customers, and a larger paying customer base. This, in turn, leads to increases in revenues that, if well managed, contribute to the financial sustainability of the utility.

- Technical assistance can play a role in helping commercial financiers adjust their lending practices by creating financial products specifically targeting the needs of the sector, including longer tenors with a sufficient grace period, and reduced collateral requirements. In doing so, commercial financiers diversify their portfolios of projects, thus reducing the risk of their overall investment portfolio risk.
- Water-related investments typically concern an investment in part of an overall system (e.g. rehabilitation of distribution infrastructure; expansion of water production or treatment facilities, etc.). How that investment is structured (e.g. what aspects of the overall system are included or not) can influence the appropriate financing structure. A common vision for impact across all stakeholders is thus key to the successful implementation of the blended finance arrangement.
- Flexible and adaptive project management is key to the smooth implementation of blended finance arrangements. Cases studied highlighted the need to continually calibrate the programmes to manage the complexity of implementing novel financing approaches in developing country contexts. In particular, delays can result from a lack of co-ordination between the stakeholders, foreign exchange negotiations, procurement issues and exogenous factors, including the readiness of capital markets.
- The effectiveness of blended finance arrangements also depends on the enabling environment in which they are implemented. Providing utilities with the financing needed to upgrade and expand their services is necessary, but it is not sufficient to make a blended finance arrangement work. Improving the enabling environment by strengthening the policy and regulatory framework as well as the institutional arrangements is equally important.

References

OECD (2018), *Making Blended Finance Work for the Sustainable Development Goals*, OECD Publishing, Paris, https://dx.doi.org/10.1787/9789264288768-en. [2]

Republic of Benin (2019), *PROJET D'ASSAINISSEMENT PLUVIAL DE LA VILLE DE COTONOU(PAPC)*, http://documents.worldbank.org/curated/en/529641552297946808/pdf/PAPC-RAPPORT-Cadre-de-Politique-de-R-installation-Vf.pdf (accessed on 14 June 2019). [4]

WHO/UNICEF (2019), *Data | JMP*, https://washdata.org/data (accessed on 8 July 2019). [3]

World Bank (2006), *The Challenge of Reducing Non-Revenue Water (NRW) in Developing Countries How the Private Sector Can Help: A Look at Performance-Based Service Contracting*, http://ppiaf.org (accessed on 29 July 2019). [1]

3 Evidence on blended finance in small-scale off-grid sanitation, wastewater collection and treatment

This chapter presents the results of the review of small-scale off-grid sanitation, wastewater collection and treatment, including: (i) an introduction into the subsector, (ii) a commercial investor perspective on the subsector, (iii) an overview of blended finance transactions, (iv) a typology of commercial investment that could be mobilised, (v) an assessment of the impact on the poor, and (vi) subsector-specific insights. The chapter finds that the early-stage nature of many sanitation enterprises evoke the need to integrate grants and technical assistance in blended finance models to create financially sound projects which may attract commercial finance.

3.1. An introduction to small-scale off-grid sanitation

Small-scale off-grid sanitation, wastewater collection and treatment solutions aim to deliver services for the safe disposal of human urine and faeces. Off-grid solutions can include traditional and improved latrines (various kinds of pits), container based sanitation (CBS), flush toilets connected to septic tanks and various wastewater collection and treatment facilities, such as faecal sludge management technologies (FSM) (World Bank, 2019[1]).

Most developed economies in the world have water and sanitation systems that are sewered or "on-grid". That is, toilets and taps are connected to a network of pipes and pumps managed by utilities (see Chapter 2). Historically, sewered systems have been seen as the "gold standard" solution for sanitation and wastewater treatment, with off-grid or onsite sanitation largely seen as a temporary solution (Bill & Melinda Gates Foundation, 2019[2]). In addition, governments and development financers have focused on and preferred large scale infrastructure to tackle sanitation, involving the construction of wastewater treatment plants and sewer systems. However, these systems require high capital and operating expenditures and large amounts of land, energy and water. There is an additional challenge of introducing infrastructure for sewers in dense urban settings (Strande, Ronteltap and Brdjanovic, 2014[3]). Further, the expansion and development of functioning, conventional sewer networks is not likely to keep pace with the rapid urban expansion typical of low and middle-income countries. Over half of the world's population now lives in urban areas and that number is increasing rapidly (UN DESA, 2018[4]).

The urgent need for sanitation solutions and the impracticality of delivering sewered sanitation coupled with technological developments has led to an increased focus on off-grid sanitation as a viable long term solution. The development of new technologies and improvements in human waste containment, transport, and decentralised treatment mean that small-scale off-grid sanitation can offer low cost solutions to meet sanitation needs (Bill & Melinda Gates Foundation, 2019[2]). Indeed, many of the social enterprises in operation in the off-grid sanitation sector offer solutions at a fraction of the cost of developing a sewered system (The Stone Family Foundation, 2014[5]). Indeed, in urban areas, dependent upon local conditions, off-grid FSM technologies can be provided for 20% of conventional sanitation costs per household (Dodane et al., 2012[6]).

At the same time, off-grid sanitation approaches can be viewed as complementary to traditional sewer systems rather than as an alternative. They can and should be designed and supported to deliver equivalent service levels to households. As such, actors in the field such as the Bill & Melinda Gates Foundation (BMGF) promote decentralised efforts alongside sewered systems. In practice, this has approach has been pursued in several countries. For example, FSM has been successfully delivered alongside sewered sanitation in Japan (Gaulke, 2006[7]). More recently, in 2017, the World Bank launched the second Ethiopia and Urban Water Supply Sanitation Project, which supports a mix of off-grid and sewered sanitation solutions (World Bank, 2017[8]). These developments highlight that there is often no single simple solution to urban sanitation problems and innovative and cohesive responses are needed that consider the whole sanitation service chain. However, the absence of institutional and regulatory arrangements for managing and monitoring the quality off-grid sanitation systems in many developing countries remains a challenge (Bernal et al., 2012[9]).

3.2. Investment profile: an assessment of the risks, returns and project attributes

In order to facilitate commercial investment in the off-grid sanitation subsector, blended finance actors on the development side need to understand the perspective and concerns of commercial investors. Ultimately, any blended finance approach should be a temporary approach to build markets that promote sustainable financing arrangements, which may include appealing investment opportunities for commercial investment in the long-run. In the following section, relevant investment parameters such as revenue and risks are assessed, as well as other relevant project attributes in order to better understand the potential role the commercial sector can play and how blended finance can facilitate such engagement. Table 3.1 summarises these investment attributes for the subsector.

Compared to other subsectors, off-grid sanitation service providers often deliver services for low-income households at an early or pioneer stage, operating on a small scale. Despite a number of social enterprises in operation for a number of years (World Bank, 2019), many businesses are employing innovative technologies that are at a nascent stage. For example, CBS solutions have been developed by social enterprises, including several variations of which have collectable waste which can be reused for other purposes. However, a recent World Bank report finds that none of the enterprises reviewed were able to fully recover costs from revenues. In addition, the report concludes that the situation was likely to persist despite efforts to reduce costs and increase revenues (World Bank, 2019[10]). Similar cost recovery challenges are faced by FSM solutions.

Table 3.1. Summary of investment attributes

Feature	Description
	Risk
Macroeconomic and business risks	Currency risk (due to mismatch revenue and debt servicing currency), market risk (demand for service), operating risk (weak performance of sanitation service providers), liquidity risk (inability to exit/sell).
Regulatory and political risks	Regulatory risk (e.g. in many developing country contexts there is no regulatory environment for off-grid sanitation), political risk (in the case of government procurement contracts) and utilities may not have mandate to engage in non-sewered sanitation).
Technical risks	Performance risk and obsolesce of utilised technology as off-grid sanitation approaches are as CBS solutions and FSM technologies are relatively new.
Environmental/ social risk	Environmental risk (e.g. chances of spillages of excreta of CBS and onsite sanitation).
	Return
Cash-flow generation	Depending on off-grid sanitation model, cash flows are generated through the sale of toilets (usually paid monthly), collection fees for waste, from products sold after processing of waste, user fees for toilets and concession contracts from local governments.
Developmental return	Can reduce levels of open defecation and improve hygiene of households leading to reduced illness. Sanitation services also and improves menstrual hygiene management (which, in turn, can reduce drop-out rates of girls in schools). Properly managed waste reduces the environmental impact of poorly managed sanitation.
	Project attributes
Greenfield vs. brownfield	Greenfield projects face additional business or technical risk due to the construction.
Scalability	Off-grid sanitation models can be scaled in particular if they are seen complementary to sewered systems and as such can access a stable revenue source, e.g. a public off-taker. Any replication of project hence depends on the underlying jurisdiction and context.
Size	Small scale direct investment in enterprises.
Transaction costs	High, given the opacity of small business typically low level of expertise in financing this sector.
Tenor/ Longevity	Varies, with the need for long term patient capital to develop and scale business models.

Source: Authors.

Revenue streams for off-grid sanitation are, as in any other sector, the key ingredient to financial sustainability. Specific to this sector, they are challenging to materialise. Blended finance can de-risk transactions and (re-)attribute cash flows but it cannot replace business models that do not have clear revenue proposition or that fail to capture economic value (Larrea, 2019[11]).

A variety of business models operate along the off-grid sanitation service chain (Figure 3.1). As a result, enterprises that are providing services in this area generate revenue streams using a variety of approaches. At the upper end spectrum of stable and sizable revenues are service-level contracts with local or national governments (e.g. utilities), which can contribute to financial sustainability. Municipal government procurement contracts can serve as a source of stable long-term revenue streams, but require a certain scale and level of profitability *ex ante*. These engagements are associated with political risk related to government payment. A recent example is Loowatt, a UK headquartered company that produces waterless sealable toilets, which reached sufficient scale to successfully bid for a procurement contract for bulk sale of toilets to a utility in the Philippines.

Figure 3.1.Potential revenues along the off-grid sanitation value chain

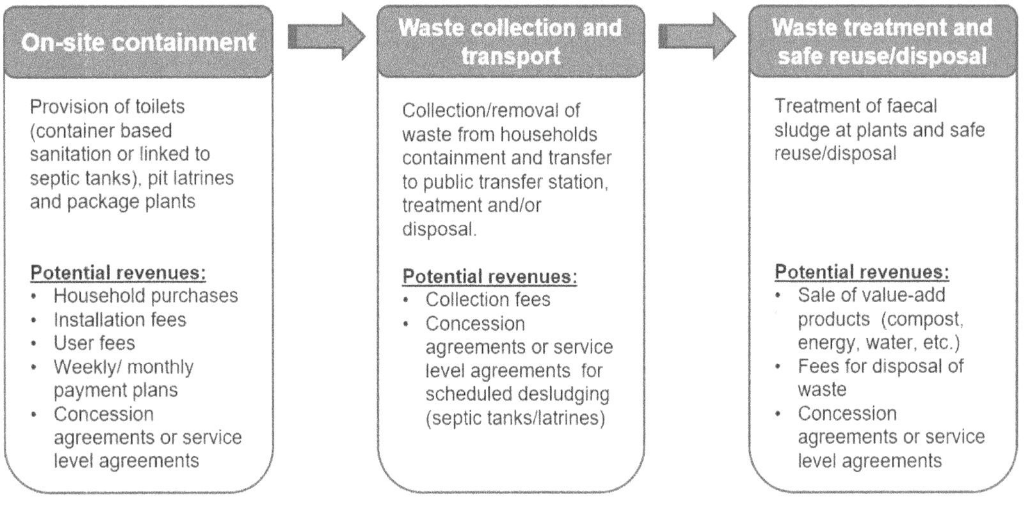

Source: Authors.

Other revenue models work bottom-up, by collecting user fees, as it is the case with CBS companies that provide container toilets to households. Toilets are provided to households and then costs are recovered through user fees charged for the operation of toilets. For example, Clean Team Toilets in Ghana provides in-home toilets to Ghanaians in Kumasi and charges a fee to households for the collection and disposal of waste (Clean Team Toilets, 2019[12]). For a weekly fee (which is estimated to be substantially lower than the cost monthly use of public toilets), users are provided with a toilet with no *ex ante* capital expenditure. In addition, the toilet does not require water or electricity to operate. While these examples are promising, overall, the number of CBS companies in operation in developing countries seems to be limited.

A more traditional source of revenue for the water and sanitation sector, taxation, can also be used to fund off-grid sanitation, mobilise finance, and spur the involvement of local private sector actors. For example, in the towns of Wai and Sinnar in India, integrated faecal sludge collection and treatment systems were partially funded by revenues from a ring-fenced sanitation tax integrated as part of an existing property tax levied by the municipal governments. Revenues from the tax allowed the municipal government to offer a concession contract to a local company on a pay-for-success basis for scheduled desludging. In addition, FSM treatment plants in both towns have been developed.

The collection of faecal sludge and desludging of septic tanks are another area of business that can provide stable revenue streams. Research into the business case for faecal sludge in Sub-Saharan African and South-East Asia has indicated that the scale of operations and the size of collection trucks can have a large impact on the profitability of small businesses operating in the market (Chowdhry and Kone, 2012[13]). Businesses have relatively high capital costs in the initial purchase of trucks, but can have regular revenue streams with scheduled desludging operations either with a service level agreement with a municipality or by charging collection fees from users. While the waste collection enterprises in the case studies reviewed in this report are currently reliant on a concession contract from municipal government, there are on-going discussions exploring the potential of development impact bonds and private financing to scale up this model.

At the end of the sanitation value chain, transported sludge must be safely disposed of. Faecal sludge treatment plants (FSTPs) can generate revenues from fees for the disposal of waste from government procurement contracts for treatment services, or from the sale of waste reuse by-products. FSTPs and the innovative technologies in operation to process waste usually consist of two processes: (1) the separation of solid and liquids and (2) the treatment of the sludge generated from the initial treatment (Singh et al., 2017[14]). Additionally, the process to treat liquids should be taken into account. The appropriate technology to process faecal sludge after primary treatment and ultimately the end products sold for reuse are determined by a number of factors, including the characteristics of sludge. These characteristics can significantly vary depending on storage and location, feasible markets for reuse products and the frequency of sludge collection (Singh et al., 2017[14]). The products derived from treated faecal sludge (dependent on the technology) can include, for example: animal feed, biogas from anaerobic digestion, and compost. Different technologies often have different land requirements, capital expenditure (CAPEX) and operational expenditure (OPEX) costs. A high level of technical skill is required to develop and operate these technologies. To date, revenue streams from FSTPs have often generated only sufficient revenue to cover operating costs. However, once these technologies have been proven and have a more established performance track record, there is the potential for these models to be scaled, though reaching profitability may not be a consequence.

Implicit benefits (see also Chapter 4 on landscape-based approaches) have the potential to unlock funding from commercial actors. For example, the Hindustan Zinc Limited (HZL), a subsidiary of Verdanta, owns and operates a zinc mine in Udaipur. It funded 95% (approximately USD 4 million) of the project cost of a FSTP in the city. The remaining 5% was provided by the municipal government in form of land acquired for the project. HZL implicitly benefits as a local stakeholder from the effective treatment of faecal sludge in the area, as HZL headquarters are situated within the region alongside other extensive resources.

Cross-subsidisation between revenue-generating treatment services and cash-flow limited off-grid sanitation models can serve as a pathway to overall financial sustainability. For example, Sanergy, takes a full value chain approach to sanitation (Sanergy, 2019[15]). The company, headquartered in Kenya, builds toilets with waste cartridges that are collected on a regular basis and then processed to produce fertilizer and animal feed (World Bank, 2019[10]). The toilets are provided to franchisees for an installation fee in addition to an annual renewal fee as well as a monthly collection fee charged to landlords. At the same time, the enterprise is processing waste into fertiliser and animal feed. Sanergy divides its business into two arms: the non-profit sanitation provision service and the for-profit waste treatment and reuse business. This is in part because the company views sanitation as a public good and the financial reality that they currently do not envision a sustainable way to provide CBS solutions at scale. This non-profit sanitation provision service arm of Sanergy pays a fee to waste treatment arm for every kilogram of faeces removed. This fee is set below market rate (World Bank, 2019[10]). As the business scales and profitability improves, a fully integrated model across the full value chain could have the potential to lead towards financial sustainability for the full range of activities (Box 3.1 provides further details on the profitability of a current sanitation business model).

Moreover, enterprises operating in the sanitation sector often face the dual challenge of the serving underdeveloped markets and also creating revenue-generating demand for their products and services (The Stone Family Foundation, 2014[5]). Beyond financial solutions, this requires advocacy in behavioural changes to build long term demand and sustainable business models.

Box 3.1. An analysis of the profit and loss factors for an exemplary sanitation business

An analysis of the profit and loss (P&L) factors for an exemplary sanitation business clearly shows the challenges to attract commercial finance, and at the same time underlines the need for blended structures to scale grant-based business models.

Sanergy have developed a toilet that captures waste in cartridges and has been in operation since 2010. These cartridges are regularly collected and sent to processing facilities to produce fertilizer and animal feed. The toilet and waste collection services provided by Sanergy are used by approximately 90 000 residents per day, with over 2 250 toilets in 2019 (Sanergy, 2019[15]). The estimated total annual cost of both the for-profit and non-profit business was estimated to be approximately USD 1.5 million in 2017. Only 19% of total costs or USD 290 000 were recovered via fees from operators or the sale of reuse product. In terms of the for-profit arm, from March 2016-17 Sanergy has sold approximately 550 tons of soil fertiliser equivalent to about USD 220 000 (World Bank, 2019[16]). The cost of waste collection from January to April 2017 was between USD 0.06 to USD 0.07 per kilogram – approximately double the amount charged to the non-profit arm for collection. An average of 13 tons of faeces and urine combined was collected per day in the first quarter of 2017 and revenues were equivalent to 40% the cost of processing (World Bank, 2019[16]). Sanergy is currently developing the use of black soldier fly larvae to produce animal feed on an industrial scale. The enterprise intends to expand its operations significantly to over 13 000 toilets in 2023. It is estimated this expansion will take 7 years and with increasing cost recovery will reduce the per person subsidy for the toilets from USD 19 to USD 2 in 2020.

Source: (World Bank, 2019[16]), Evaluating the Potential of Container-Based Sanitation: Sanergy in Nairobi, Kenya, http://documents.worldbank.org/curated/en/661201550180019891/Evaluating-the-Potential-of-Container-Based-Sanitation-Sanergy-in-Nairobi-Kenya & (Sanergy, 2019[15]), http://www.sanergy.com

3.3. Blended finance instruments and mechanisms for financing small scale off-grid sanitation

Research, interviews and case studies undertaken for this report indicate that opportunities for blended finance transactions are often limited at this stage, with many development actors focusing on helping enterprises scale and become investable.

Grant funding dominates the development finance approaches in the subsector. Philanthropic organisations like the Stone Family Foundation (SFF) provide risk capital to enterprises providing off-grid sanitation services. For example, SFF has provided USD 2 million of grant funding for the non-profit arm of Sanergy from 2016-19 (The Stone Family Foundation, 2019[17]). Indeed, the majority of funding for the non-profit business arm which provides and installs toilets comes from 15 family and corporate foundations (World Bank, 2019[16]).

Grant funding can indeed support the scaling of new and innovative business models. Loowatt received funding to pilot and scale the operation of its waterless toilet from the Bill & Melinda Gates Foundation (BMGF), initially as part of the "Reinvent the Toilet" initiative in 2011 and received a further grant from the foundation of over USD 1.2 million in 2013 (Bill and Melinda Gates Foundation, 2018[18]). This provided the company with funding to develop the technology, attract further funding and undertake a successful pilot of the waterless public toilets. An important part of Loowatt's growth has been through working with utilities to deliver whole value chain CBS. In 2016, Loowatt began co-operating with utilities in both the UK and Madagascar. The success in Madagascar and London allowed Loowatt to participate in the pilot scheme for Laguna Water in Manila funded through the Urban Sanitation Challenge (see Box 3.2). Loowatt was subsequently tendered to provide bulk toilets to the utility.

Grant funding is also relevant for project design, research and feasibility studies. For example, a USD 1 million grant from BMGF was influential in helping the Centre for Policy Research in India to provide reports and technical assistance to the state and local government in Maharashtra. This ultimately led to the development of a USD 30 million sewerage treatment plant project in Udaipur, funded by the private company Vedanta and built on government land.

In addition, USD 1 million grant funding from BMGF along with technical advice and research from the Centre for Environmental Planning and Technology (CEPT) University Centre for Water and Sanitation were critical to the municipal government agreeing to implement integrated faecal sludge management pilots. The grant enabled CEPT to undertake the prerequisite research and provide assistance to the municipalities on the implementation of the sanitation tax as well as the development of faecal sludge treatment plants.

Technical assistance is playing a critical role in the development of early stage of social enterprises in the subsector. For example, Sanivation, a social enterprise operating in Kenya, developed a faecal waste disposal system that transforms waste into fuel briquettes with technical assistance and grants from USAID and the US Centre for Disease Control (CDC) (USAID, 2019[19]). The fuel briquettes produced by the technology provide a cleaner alternative to charcoal and other fuels. The CDC supported the pilot of the project in 2013 and the project received additional grant funding and technical assistance from USAID to develop and scale up operations of the FSTP.

Concessional financing is currently targeting the treatment dimension in this subsector. Sanivation is a good example of how grant funding and technical assistance can spur and develop innovative ideas so that concessional financing can be attracted. This financing can take the form of patient capital that has a long-term horizon and requires a social return in addition to a financial return (see also (OECD, 2019[20])). In 2017, USAID's Development Innovation Ventures program provided additional funding to Sanivation to help mobilise additional finance for project growth. This funding is projected to continue until 2020 (USAID Water Team, 2018[21]). FINCA Ventures invested patient capital in Sanivation in 2018 (FINCA Ventures, 2018[22]). Also, Acumen patient capital to the for-profit arm of Sanergy to scale up its operations for excrement management and the production of fertiliser and animal feed (Acumen, 2019[23]). In addition, Sanergy has attracted *non-concessional* development finance from OPIC in the form of a USD 5 million loan for a new animal feed production facility (OPIC, 2017[24]).

Microfinance can serve as a tool to provide access to finance to access off-grid sanitation assets. An example of the use of grant funding to scale an organisation and mobilise commercial finance is the USD 240 000 grant to Gramalaya by Water.org to pilot WASH microfinancing in 2007 (Water.org, 2013[25]) (for more information on Water.org's sanitation microfinance programme see Box 3.3). This allowed Gramalaya to develop a WASH-focused microfinance institution (MFI), Gramalaya Urban and Rural Development Initiatives and Network (GUARDIAN). At inception, GUARDIAN was the only MFI in India that focused solely on water and sanitation engaging in micro-lending to households to support the purchase of water and sanitation assets at a household level such as toilet construction, rainwater harvesting equipment and household water purifiers. As a result of grant funding, GUARDIAN was able to mobilise commercial financing from a local public-sector bank, the Indian Overseas Bank and social investors Acumen and Milaap (Share, 2012[26]). The risk-return relationship of microfinance exposures in this area strictly depends on the project the loan proceeds are used for. As described before, the loan-financed projects are not necessarily productive investments. A study of three case studies by the World Bank in 2015 indicates that the default risk for micro-loans targeted at WASH is comparable to micro-loans for other sectors (Ikeda and Arney, 2015[27]).

Box 3.2. Water.org's WaterCredit initiative

Mainstreaming micro-lending for water and sanitation

WaterCredit works with local financial institutions. Under most circumstances, these institutions already lend to low-income people but are reluctant to lend specifically for water and/or sanitation due to perceptions of high repayment risk. The WaterCredit structure is designed to encourage these institutions to pilot water and sanitation lending.

The strategic use of technical assistance and/or a small grant from Water.org's philanthropic donors for project preparation – market assessment, loan product development, borrower education materials, marketing collateral, etc. – aims increasing the outreach of sanitation services by mobilising household and commercial finance. In exchange for this assistance, the institution commits to loan targets within a given timeframe. During project preparation, tailored water and/or sanitation loan products are being developed. The institution is responsible for sourcing its capital for on-lending. The MFIs provide borrowers with educational materials alongside their loans. The clients then use the loan proceeds to purchase or construct the water or sanitation asset.

Institutions report to Water.org on progress against the agreed-upon targets. Verification checks that the structure was built are done on an interval basis by third parties, and Water.org staff also conduct regular monitoring visits to assess progress and provide guidance.

Figure 3.2. The WaterCredit Financing Structure

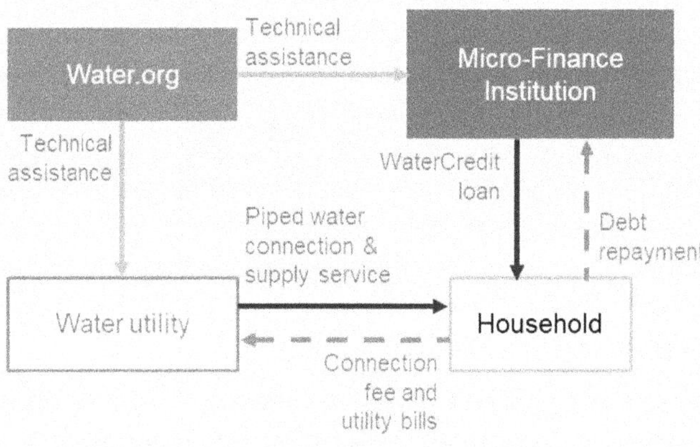

Source: Authors.

Given the small scale of most off-grid sanitation enterprises and financiers and their relatively small, tailor-made needs for external financing, *portfolio approaches* to financing a variety of such enterprises may serve as a means to mobilise commercial investment in the future. For example, WaterEquity is a fund manager conceived of and incubated by Water.org. It is now a separate entity with the purpose of mobilising commercial capital for water and sanitation financiers and enterprises in emerging markets. WaterEquity disburses loans to MFIs and, increasingly, small and medium enterprises, for water and sanitation lending. While participation in Water.org's WaterCredit programme helps to identify MFIs with demonstrable track records of operating in the water and sanitation sector (see also Chapter 2), WaterEquity investments extend beyond the WaterCredit network. As of April 2019, WaterEquity manages two funds: the USD 33 million WaterCredit Investment Fund 3 and the USD 50 million Flagship Fund

(WaterEquity, 2018[28]). Concessional capital providers include Bank of America, providing an USD 5 million loan with zero interest rate (America, 2017[29]), OPIC providing in total USD 20 million, as well as the Conrad N. Hilton, Skoll Foundation and Osprey Foundation (OPIC, 2019[30]).

Further pay-for-success instruments are such as *Development Impact Bonds (DIBs)* are being explored. In 2018, the first sanitation impact bond was launched in India. Initially the bond started with a pilot phase of EUR 5 million but aims to raise EUR 100 million from institutional investors in three years (Dutch Water Sector, 2018[31]). The funds raised from the bond will be on-lent to Indian MFIs that will then disburse sanitation loans to households for the construction of toilets. The partners of the bond include Dutch institutional investors, Actiam a Dutch impact investor, KMPG, Waste and Indian MFIs. MFIs will repay investors, including a small a financial return provided by Actiam (Dutch Water Sector, 2018[31]). A result-based financing element is incorporated: if the targeted level of 1.5 million toilets is reached, the MFIs will be rewarded with lower interest rates. It is, however, important that increases in household toilet provision is linked to complimentary interventions such as faecal sludge treatment systems.

Projects exploring the potential of other pay-for-success instruments in water and sanitation such as social impact incentives (SIINCs), which directly reward high-impact enterprises with premium payments for achieving social results, are also currently being explored by the Swiss Development and Cooperation (SDC) Agency and Roots of Impact (Waterpreneurs, 2018[32]). However, currently the use of pay-for-success instruments in the water and sanitation sector are for the most part in the project development stage.

Social Finance is currently undertaking feasibility studies into the potential use of the DIBs to fund non-networked sanitation treatment of faecal sludge (Social Finance, 2018[33]). There still often remains a challenge that poorer households in developing countries cannot afford collections and fees, and as a result only sludge that is created by households who can afford to pay for it is treated. The creation of DIBs creates an opportunity to change incentives to ensure that poorer households also have access to faecal sludge services while it also remains profitable for businesses that operate faecal sludge treatment processes. Similarly, the success of pay-for-results contracts for small companies to undertake scheduled desludging in the Indian towns Wai and Sinnar has led to research and discussion with CEPT University, Social Finance and impact investors about the potential for DIBs to be used to scale up services. Research and discussions into the potential of DIBs in this area is ongoing.

3.4. A typology of investors in small-scale off-grid sanitation

Foundation and venture philanthropy are providing grants, technical assistance and concessional finance to help service providers reach scale and transition towards a sustainable business model that attracts the private sector. The major philanthropic funders of the water sector primarily focus efforts into subsectors that address drinking water supply, sanitation services and related research. But, they also fund water projects that relate to livelihoods, conservation, disaster relief, policy and administration and health education. BMGF is a frequent outlier in terms of funding, supporting only urban sanitation-related efforts. In comparison, the Coca-Cola Foundation places a larger focus on environmental elements with funding for river basin development and water resources conservation.

Non-governmental organisations like Water.org also active in the subsector. Water.org provides technical assistance and grants to MFIs to enable them to expand existing sanitation loan portfolios or develop new sanitation loan products to low income households. For example the WaterCredit initiative (explored in greater detail in Box 3.2) encourages the disbursement of microloans earmarked for water and sanitation projects by covering the costs of the project preparation phase.

Development agencies as USAID or the Swiss SDC provide grant funding for innovative business models in the sanitation sector.

Social and impact investors who aim to achieve a social as well as a financial return are a source of finance that could potentially be mobilised further. Many impact investors already have investments in the WASH sector. Examples of impact investors active in the subsector include FINCA Ventures and Acumen. According to the Global Impact Investing Network's (GIIN) Annual Impact Investor Survey 2018, a quarter of impact investors surveyed invest in water and sanitation. However, in terms of volume, this represents only 4% of total assets under management – an equivalent to USD 9.12 billion. In addition, a group of impact investors and entrepreneurs have convened to form Waterpreneurs and have created a platform, Innovate4Water, to bring together social enterprises, entrepreneurs and small and large scale investors to invest in water and sanitation. Innovate4Water is working as part of the Accelerate2030: Access to Clean Water and Sanitation formed by the UNDP and Impact hub. Accelerate2030 works to scale up the impact of social enterprises working to address the SDGs 6 (Accelerate2030, 2019[34]).

Development Finance Institutions (DFIs) such as OPIC provide non-concessional development finance to mobilise private capital. Thus far, DFIs have focused on the business models or areas that have clearer revenue streams such as wastewater treatment that leads to the production of energy or animal feed that can be sold, as in the case of Sanergy, for instance, as highlighted the previous section. This is in line with DFIs' ambition and mandate to be profitable and financially sustainable. At the same time, DFIs could explore blended concessional finance models that aim at scaling holistic business models that integrate activities across the sanitation value chain. Scaling inputs – the non-profitable sanitation services – to ultimately achieve higher revenues from the fertiliser/animal feed production could be financed by blended models that combine different return expectations.

Corporates can contribute to the development and scaling up of off-grid sanitation and whole value chain approaches to sanitation, though not necessarily by investing at commercial rates. Indeed, Unilever, Veolia, Kimberly Clark, and Firmenich are part of the Toilet Board Coalition (TBC) launched in 2014 alongside the World Bank, USAID, the Department for International Development (DFID), AFD, Water.org and others (Toilet Board Coalition, 2019[35]). TBC is a business-led platform that seeks to enable private sector engagement in the sanitation sector by connecting large and small companies. TBC launched an accelerator in 2016 to scale up innovative solutions to sanitation and whole value chain approaches to sanitation. Thus far, the accelerator has helped over ten social enterprises including Sanivation and Sanergy. Beyond this, commercial finance from actors such as banks or institutional investors is largely absent for off-grid sanitation services thus far.

3.5. An assessment of the sustainable development impact

Projects and enterprises providing off-grid sanitation services can have a direct impact on improving water and sanitation outcomes in areas or for people who do not have access to sewered sanitation. Social enterprises that provide CBS solutions can have a positive impact on the health and hygiene of the households and communities they serve by safely sealing excreta and removing it for treatment. Improved sanitation delivers multiple benefits such as lower disease burden, healthier living environments and social and economic gains more broadly (World Bank, 2019[16]). CBS solutions can provide safe services comparable to flush toilets and the products of whole sanitation value chain models were also found to be safe (World Bank, 2019[16]). In addition, the Container Based Alliance is working to adopt the World Health Organisation's Sanitation Safety Plan. In contrast to pit latrines, CBS solutions can still be used during floods.

While the current scale of CBS solutions is small, they are an elementary part of a portfolio of solutions in urban areas to provide city-wide inclusive sanitation. In particular, in water scarce areas and areas where little space is available, CBS can offer relatively affordable sanitation solutions. That is, revenue models that charge a fee for toilet use or collection offer more flexible repayment plans, with monthly repayment schemes that can smooth costs out overtime for users and hence increase accessibility (World Bank, 2019[16]).

The introduction of an integrated faecal sludge collection and treatment systems produces tangible benefits for households, the community and the environment. For instance, in the case of the municipalities Wai and Sinnar in India interventions resulted in increased access to such desludging services for 1 500 properties. There was an acceptance rate of over 93% from households for the scheduled service. The funding of the system was sourced via a sanitation tax implemented as part of the property tax. To mitigate the impact on poorer households, the tax is designed to be progressive. As a result, smaller properties pay less. Indeed, the incremental payments and scheduled desludging has made the service more affordable to households, with some paying one-fifth of what they paid previously. The success of the Wai and Sinnar pilots has the potential to have a broader impacts across Maharashtra. Findings from the pilots will inform state-wide efforts to develop regulatory frameworks and policies to overcome barriers to sanitation service provision.

Microfinance loans to households for the purchase of onsite sanitation have potential to both increase access to finance and to water and sanitation services for low income households. Research undertaken, including randomised control trials, indicates that there is demand amongst households for sanitation products provided they can meet affordability constraints and spread the cost of investments overtime (Trémolet, Goufrane and Muruka, 2015[36]). For example, the majority of WaterCredit's borrowers in Bangladesh have per capita income below USD 6 dollars (Water.org, 2018[37]). Indeed, MFIs that provide sanitation loans report strong demand (Trémolet and Kumar, 2013[38]). However, there is some concern about affordability for households to pay loans back for investments that are not productive. MFI sanitation loans can be income enhancing by potentially reducing medical expenses and days lost to illness, time saved through convenience contributing towards increase productivity. At the same time, there is no causal link to increased income, so borrowers are reliant on existing income to repay loans (Trémolet, Goufrane and Muruka, 2015[36]). Indeed, a recent 2018 evaluation of the WaterCredit's programmes operations in Bangladesh found that of the 58% of loans used for sanitation improvements 94% of sanitation facilities were in good condition (Water.org, 2018[37]). In conclusion, access to finance for sanitation may not be suitable for the poorest of the poor who may need to be served by traditional aid and philanthropy.

While the use and implementation of pay-for-success instruments is still at a fledgling stage, DIBs and SIINCs can provide a mechanism to increase sanitation services provided to the households at base of the pyramid. For example, currently many of the lowest income households in developing countries are unable to afford collection and tipping fees for excreta and subsequently their waste is not effectively treated. A DIB or SIINC could realign incentives by making payments dependent on increased collections or provision of services to the base of pyramid – in effect subsidising the coverage of the poorest households unable to afford sanitation services.

3.6. Subsector-specific insights

Improving access to sanitation is crucial for sustainable development. The off-grid sanitation subsector is driven by small scale businesses that are associated with relatively high risk due to rather new technologies and their need for long-term capital. At this stage, these characteristics are not matching commercial investors' preferences.

- The commercial investment perspective on small-scale off-grid sanitation is not appealing at this stage. Small, early-stage enterprises with innovative but nascent business models operating in the subsector present (1) limited capital absorption capacity and hence require commercial investment at small scale, (2) present higher risk due to partially unproven technologies, (3) underline the importance of long-term equity investment or even venture capital in order to prove and scale the business models.

- Blended finance models to unlock commercial investment have not yet emerged. Commercial finance from banks or investments from asset managers is largely absent from the subsector at present due to the aforementioned investment characteristics. Philanthropic actors such as BMGF or the Stone Family Foundation and social impact investors play a major role in providing grant funding or concessional finance in this subsector. At the same time, innovative financing models such as DIBs are increasingly explored to attract additional finance, for instance by Social Value UK.
- Grant funding appears to go to a handful of sanitation enterprises. The good practice examples of innovative business models examined in this publication are receiving funding often from a variety of different international actors. The typical innovative business model is the provision of CBS solutions that seek to address the whole sanitation value chain (e.g. have collectable waste cartridges that are processed and the resulting products sold). Thus far, CBS models have not reached scale even with grant funding.
- An observed pathway to sustainable revenue for the off-grid sanitation subsector is to collaborate with water utilities and governments at a local and national level. Procurement contracts offer the opportunity for enterprises to scale operations and provide a stable revenue source. For example, Loowatt, through its co-operation with the utility Laguna Water in Manila, is expected to receive a procurement contract for bulk sale of toilets, with the potential for sales on a larger scale in the future. Another example of a potential pathway to scale off-grid sanitation is the implementation of the ring-fenced sanitation tax in the towns of Wai and Sinnar. The partnership with state and local governments and revenues from the tax helped increase access to sanitation services by funding faecal sludge collection and treatment systems. The State Government plans to scale operations across more than 300 cities in Maharashtra.
- Another approach is to focus on end-users. Microfinance can increase access to sanitation by providing low income households access to finance. Blended loans and credit lines to MFIs can work to increase the demand for sanitation services and assets and hence indirectly support scaling of sanitation enterprises.
- Blended concessional finance can offer a pathway into beyond-grant models and help build local markets. Blended finance aims to ultimately mobilise commercial investment to increase the volumes of finance available for sustainable development. Guarantees, loan syndications or equity investment priced at market rates can be effective. A concessional element is not a conditional requirement to that respect. From a commercial perspective, what matters is whether an investment opportunity meets the commercial investor's investment criteria, regardless of concessional finance involved. In the sanitation subsector, a concessionality element may work towards building the market and to help enterprises achieve scale and ultimately attract commercial finance. That is, government or philanthropic grant facilities could be blended with development or commercial actors' resources to generate investment opportunities in the long run.
- Developing holistic financing approaches for integrated business models that link the provision of sanitation services with complementary wastewater collection and treatment service could help to scale the delivery of off-grid sanitation services by attracting more commercial finance. Blended finance models may play a role in strategically valuing business models across the supply chain. This may include grants or soft term loans blended with loans at commercial rates. For example, the enterprise Sanergy operates across the sanitation value chain by providing sanitation services as well as faecal sludge treatment services. While philanthropic actors are providing grant funding for the sanitation non-profit pillar, DFIs are providing loans to the for-profit sludge treatment and reuse department. Holistic blended financing models could bring the two sides together by using philanthropic or government grant funding in blended models to support the underlying sanitation business.

- Developing a portfolio of projects can address unfavourable project attributes. Providing commercial investors the access to a variety of different transactions in the sanitation sector can mitigate concerns around small ticket size, risk exposure as well as high transaction cost. Pooling mechanisms such as blended finance funds tailor different risk and return profiles for individual investors, with development financiers often taking fist loss and junior traches buffering the risk for more commercial investors in the senior tranches. Moreover, guarantees can strategically mitigate portfolio risk. In the sanitation market, private equity funds providing early stage capital or expansion financing could address a seemingly "missing middle" between grant funding and concessional debt financing.
- A conducive policy and regulatory framework is needed in order for small-scale off-grid sanitation approaches to achieve scale and provide clarity for investors. Unclear and underdeveloped legal frameworks can hinder the development of the market. As a result, in some cases enterprises are unable to sell reuse produce of faecal sludge (compost, fertiliser, etc.) on open markets because the necessary legal framework does not exist.

References

Accelerate2030 (2019), *Accelerate2030 | Scaling Impact Globally*, https://accelerate2030.net/ (accessed on 14 June 2019). [34]

Acumen (2019), *Acumen | Sanergy*, https://acumen.org/investment/sanergy/ (accessed on 14 June 2019). [23]

America, B. (2017), *Investing in clean water and sanitation to address needs among world's poor*, https://about.bankofamerica.com/en-us/what-guides-us/water-equity.html#fbid=2NfjPwAcmmU (accessed on 14 June 2019). [29]

Bernal, D. et al. (2012), *Key issues for decentralization in municipal wastewater treatment*, https://hal-enpc.archives-ouvertes.fr/hal-00731140 (accessed on 29 July 2019). [9]

Bill & Melinda Gates Foundation (2019), *Water, Sanitation & Hygiene - Strategy Overview*, https://www.gatesfoundation.org/What-We-Do/Global-Growth-and-Opportunity/Water-Sanitation-and-Hygiene (accessed on 11 April 2019). [2]

Bill and Melinda Gates Foundation (2018), *Loowatt Ltd. - Bill & Melinda Gates Foundation*, https://www.gatesfoundation.org/How-We-Work/Quick-Links/Grants-Database/Grants/2013/07/OPP1083134 (accessed on 25 April 2019). [18]

Chowdhry, S. and D. Kone (2012), *Business Analysis of Fecal Sludge Management: Emptying and Transportation Services in Africa and Asia Draft Final Report Sangeeta Chowdhry and Doulaye Kone*, Bill and Melinda Gates Foundation, http://www.susana.org/_resources/documents/default/2-1662-chowdhury-2012-business.pdf (accessed on 13 June 2019). [13]

Clean Team Toilets (2019), *Clean Team Toilet -Home Page*, https://www.cleanteamtoilets.com/ (accessed on 25 April 2019). [12]

Dodane, P. et al. (2012), "Capital and operating costs of full-scale fecal sludge management and wastewater treatment systems in Dakar, Senegal.", *Environmental science & technology*, Vol. 46/7, pp. 3705-11, http://dx.doi.org/10.1021/es2045234. [6]

Dutch Water Sector (2018), *Three Dutch NGOs sign mondial agreement to scale up sanitation projects*, https://www.dutchwatersector.com/news-events/news/31666-three-dutch-ngos-sign-mondial-agreement-to-scale-up-sanitation-projects.html (accessed on 14 May 2019). [31]

FINCA Ventures (2018), *Why We Invested: Sanivation – FINCA Ventures – Medium*, https://medium.com/finca-ventures/why-we-invested-sanivation-cde4fc7cba9c (accessed on 25 April 2019). [22]

Gaulke, L. (2006), "On-site wastewater treatment and reuses in Japan", *Proceedings of the Institution of Civil Engineers - Water Management*, Vol. 159/2, pp. 103-109, http://dx.doi.org/10.1680/wama.2006.159.2.103. [7]

Ikeda, J. and H. Arney (2015), *Financing Water and Sanitation for the Poor: The role of microfinance institutions in addressing the water and sanitation gap*, World Bank, https://www.wsp.org/sites/wsp.org/files/publications/WSP-Waterdotorg-Financing-WASH-for-the-Poor-Microfinance.pdf (accessed on 25 April 2019). [27]

Larrea, J. (2019), *Key ingredient in the blended-finance blend: revenues*, https://impactalpha.com/key-ingredient-in-the-blended-finance-blend-revenues/ (accessed on 25 April 2019). [11]

OECD (2019), *Social Impact Investment 2019: The Impact Imperative for Sustainable Development*, OECD Publishing, Paris, https://dx.doi.org/10.1787/9789264311299-en. [20]

OPIC (2019), *OPIC Supports Two Projects to Expand Access to Safe Drinking Water | OPIC : Overseas Private Investment Corporation*, https://www.opic.gov/press-releases/2019/opic-supports-two-projects-expand-access-safe-drinking-water (accessed on 14 June 2019). [30]

OPIC (2017), *Sanergy Investment Overview*, https://www.opic.gov/sites/default/files/files/9000032207.pdf (accessed on 14 June 2019). [24]

Sanergy (2019), *Home - Sanergy*, http://www.sanergy.com/ (accessed on 25 April 2019). [15]

Share (2012), *Small-scale finance for water and sanitation*, https://assets.publishing.service.gov.uk/media/57a08aa3e5274a27b20006cb/EUWI_and_SHARE_report_on_small_scale_finance_in_WATSAN_April_2012.pdf (accessed on 14 June 2019). [26]

Singh, S. et al. (2017), "Technology options for faecal sludge management in developing countries: Benefits and revenue from reuse", *Environmental Technology & Innovation*, Vol. 7, pp. 203-218, http://dx.doi.org/10.1016/j.eti.2017.02.004. [14]

Social Finance (2018), *WASH in Rwanda and Senegal*, https://www.socialfinance.org.uk/projects/wash-rwanda-and-senegal (accessed on 25 April 2019). [33]

Strande, L., M. Ronteltap and D. Brdjanovic (2014), *Systems Approach for Implementation and Operation Faecal Sludge Management*, https://www.un-ihe.org/sites/default/files/fsm_book_lr.pdf (accessed on 11 April 2019). [3]

The Stone Family Foundation (2019), *Sanergy – The Stone Family Foundation*, http://www.thesff.com/water-and-sanitation/urban-sanitation-services/sanergy/ (accessed on 25 April 2019). [17]

The Stone Family Foundation (2014), *How to Spend a Penny: 10 lessons from funding market-based approaches in water, sanitation and hygiene*, http://www.thinknpc.org/publications/a-funder-journey/ (accessed on 12 April 2019). [5]

Toilet Board Coalition (2019), *About | Toilet Board*, http://www.toiletboard.org/about (accessed on 25 April 2019). [35]

Trémolet, S., M. Goufrane and G. Muruka (2015), "Microfinance for sanitation: what is needed to move to scale?", Vol. 34, pp. 1756-3488, http://dx.doi.org/10.3362/1756-3488.2015.022. [36]

Trémolet, S. and T. Kumar (2013), *Evaluating the potential of microfinance for sanitation in India*, https://assets.publishing.service.gov.uk/media/57a08a40ed915d3cfd00067a/microfinance_for_sanitation_in_India_May_2013.pdf (accessed on 7 May 2019). [38]

UN DESA (2018), *68% of the world population projected to live in urban areas by 2050*, https://www.un.org/development/desa/en/news/population/2018-revision-of-world-urbanization-prospects.html (accessed on 25 April 2019). [4]

USAID (2019), *Turning Waste into Power*, Global Waters, https://www.globalwaters.org/GWS-Stories/turning-waste-power (accessed on 25 April 2019). [19]

USAID Water Team (2018), *Trying to Solve Sanitation and Energy Problems at the Same Time*, https://medium.com/usaid-global-waters/trying-to-solve-sanitation-and-energy-problems-at-the-same-time-55e56d4e41d2 (accessed on 31 July 2019). [21]

Water.org (2018), *WaterCredit: Catalyzing access to safe drinking water and sanitation in Bangladesh*, http://www.findevgateway.org/sites/default/files/publication_files/2019-2-11_water.org_ikea_evaluation_brief.pdf (accessed on 7 May 2019). [37]

Water.org (2013), *Water, Sanitation and Microfinance Toolkits: Introduction to Opportunities in Water, Sanitation and Hygiene Finance*, https://water.org/documents/53/Water.org_Toolkit_1_-_Intro_to_Opportunities_in_WASH_Microfinance.pdf (accessed on 14 June 2019). [25]

WaterEquity (2018), *WaterEquity announces the first closing of its US $50 million impact investment fund*, https://www.prnewswire.com/news-releases/waterequity-announces-the-first-closing-of-its-us-50-million-impact-investment-fund-300716450.html (accessed on 7 May 2019). [28]

Waterpreneurs (2018), *Impact Investing for Water: Innovative Finance for Scaling-up WASH Market-Based Solutions*, https://docs.wixstatic.com/ugd/2c9167_0eed97e0992c4996b1067582bb425ca0.pdf (accessed on 25 April 2019). [32]

World Bank (2019), *Evaluating the Potential of Container-Based Sanitation: Sanergy in Nairobi, Kenya*, http://www.worldbank.org/gwsp (accessed on 23 April 2019). [10]

World Bank (2019), *Evaluating the Potential of Container-Based Sanitation: Sanergy in Nairobi, Kenya*, World Bank Water Global Practice, http://documents.worldbank.org/curated/en/661201550180019891/Evaluating-the-Potential-of-Container-Based-Sanitation-Sanergy-in-Nairobi-Kenya (accessed on 25 April 2019). [16]

World Bank (2019), *OBA Sanitation Microfinance Program*, http://documents.worldbank.org/curated/en/735481552555207449/pdf/Implementation-Completion-and-Results-Report-ICR-Document-OBA-SANITATION-MICROFINANCE-PROGRAM-P157958.pdf (accessed on 21 March 2019). [1]

World Bank (2017), *Not All Toilets Look the Same: A Peek into Citywide Inclusive Sanitation on World Toilet Day*, https://www.worldbank.org/en/news/feature/2017/11/17/world-toilet-day-2017 (accessed on 25 April 2019). [8]

4 Evidence on blended finance in multipurpose infrastructure and landscape-based approaches

This chapter presents the results of the in-depth review of multipurpose water infrastructure (MPWI) and landscape-based approaches, including: (i) an introduction into the subsector, (ii) a commercial investor perspective on the subsector, (iii) an overview of blended finance transactions, (iv) a typology of commercial investment ready to be mobilised, (v) an assessment of the impact on the poor, and (vi) subsector-specific insights. It finds that for MPWI blended finance models are an established financing instrument mobilising commercial finance at scale. For landscape-based approaches, blended finance can potentially operate as a fit-for-purpose financing instrument as it brings together different stakeholders responding to their individual investment preferences, but developments remain at a very early stage.

4.1. An introduction to multipurpose water infrastructure and landscape-based approaches

Multipurpose water infrastructure (MPWI) and landscape-based approaches refer to investments that deliver multiple water-related benefits, which can include cross-sectoral benefits such as energy production, agriculture and biodiversity conservation. MPWI can be defined as "all man-made water infrastructure, including dams, dykes, reservoirs and associated irrigation canals and water distribution networks, which are used or may be used for multiple purposes, for economic, social and environmental activities" (Naughton, DeSantis and Martoussevitch, 2017[1]). While MPWI may be designed for a single purpose, in practice, water is used in a multi-faceted way and as such, MPWI can be multi-purpose by either design or practice (Naughton, DeSantis and Martoussevitch, 2017[1]).

Landscape-based approaches refer to projects within a given spatial area (e.g. catchment or basin), which often incorporate nature-based solutions.[2] These are emerging approaches which complement traditional approaches to water-related investments that can deliver cross-sectoral benefits. These approaches may include investments to protect and manage watersheds - areas of land that drain rainwater or snow into one location such as a stream, lake or wetland (TNC, 2018[2]). They include projects that prevent pollution, hydrological risks, such as floods and droughts, erosion and run-off that negatively effects the quality and quantity of water used for drinking water supply, agriculture, industry, ecosystems and habitats. Landscape-based approaches provide a framework across entire spatial area in an integrated manner (Kissinger et al., 2013[3]).

In this chapter, select emerging examples of landscape-based approaches are discussed, recognising that experience is still preliminary and further analysis is required to more fully examine the economics and financing of such approaches and draw lessons learned.

4.2. Investment profile: an assessment of the risks, returns and project attributes

Even within the subsector of multi-purpose water infrastructure and landscape-based approaches, there is great variation in terms of project types, and as a result risk and return characteristics. Comparatively, the attribution and economic valuation of revenue streams from landscape-based approaches is more complex. In addition, multiple stakeholders and communities involved in large scale projects and projects can increase the cost and time of project delivery, but their involvement is critical to ensure that projects deliver benefits for the entire community over the long term.

Given the large size of most multipurpose water infrastructure projects, these are typically financed by setting up special purpose vehicles (SPVs) owned by a consortium of project sponsors that can raise further debt funding if needed. SPVs are set up for the sole purpose of financing, building and potentially running the infrastructure project.[3] These companies are of limited recourse to their owners' assets and

[2] Nature-based solutions (NbS) involve protecting, restoring and improving the management of ecosystems to deliver ecosystem services. NbS can also include the creation of natural processes in modified or artificial ecosystems, such as the construction of new wetlands to treat wastewater. By supporting the provision of ecosystem services, these interventions can serve as a complement to, or substitute for, the use of conventional engineered infrastructure.

[3] SPVs are playing a role also in public-private partnerships (PPPs), which refer to "an agreement between the government and one or more private partners (which may include the operators and the financers) according to which the private partners deliver the service in such a manner that the service delivery objectives of the government are aligned with the profit objectives of the private partners and where the effectiveness of the alignment depends on a sufficient transfer of risk to the private partners" (OECD, 2008[17]). Build Operate Own Transfer (BOOT) contracts are a common contractual PPP framework in the MPWI subsector. As such, financing could include blended finance approaches. For example, the Government of Lao and NTPC signed a PPP/BOOT agreement in 2002 contracting NTPC to finance, develop, construct, own, and operate the hydroelectric plant and facilities for 25 years. Similarly, the

hence depend on the quality and cash flows of the asset. As such, MPWI are not different to other infrastructure projects and hence appeal to commercial investors that seek long-term opportunities at scale.

Table 4.1. Summary of investment attributes

Feature	Description
	Risk
Macroeconomic and business risks	Currency risk (due to mismatch revenue and debt servicing currency), credit/off-taker risk (if applicable), operating risk (due to a variety of different technologies in MPWI), termination risk (risk of early termination of long-term contracts), market risk (demand for service), construction risk (if applicable).
Regulatory and political risks	Regulatory risk (e.g. change in tariffs if any; private participation in infrastructure).
Technical risks	Obsolesce of utilised technology given the long-term nature of contracts and multitude of technologies applied.
Environmental/ social risk	Environmental risk (e.g. complex and costly assessment of MPWIs adherence to environmental standards; variability of availability of water resources due to climate change can reduce performance of MPWI, for example hydropower production). Potential negative environmental impacts of large MPWI, disrupting natural flow regimes that support ecosystem services. Social risk (e.g. the resettlement of households that will be flooded down stream of dams or the impact of landscape-based approaches on communities including resettlement).
	Return
Cash-flow generation	MPWI projects often have quite clear predictable revenue streams, for example in case of electricity generation tariffs or power purchase agreements (PPAs) and large scale waste treatment plants. Cash-flows generated by landscape approaches to delivering water-related services often generate cash flows within actors operating in the spatial area, including by increasing turnover, efficiencies or reducing cost and expenditures of e.g. bulk water supply.
Developmental return	Projects can have potentially significant economic effect on areas. Landscape-based approaches can improved water management and quality for downstream users.
	Project attributes
Greenfield vs. brownfield	Greenfield projects face additional business or technical risk due to the construction.
Scalability	MPWI and landscape-based approaches are significantly dependent (by definition) on the spatial area where they are located, including the actors located in the areas. At the same time, in particular landscape-based approaches such as water funds have proven to be scalable and replicable when adapted to the local context.
Size	MPWI are typically large scale projects run as Special Purpose Vehicles (SPVs). Landscape infrastructure projects tend to be smaller focusing on spatial area.
Transaction costs	Adapting projects to the local context comes with high project development cost.
Tenor / Longevity	Long tenor of in particular MPWI public private partnerships (PPPs), e.g. 20-25 years.

Source: Authors.

Commercial investors value projects with a power element, such as hydropower production, in part because of the predictable business case of revenue streams associated with such infrastructure projects. That is, tariffs and power purchase agreements (PPAs) for electricity produced can provide private investors with a clear idea of the project funding. For example, the Kalangala Infrastructure Services SPV, a MPWI project providing transport, water piping, wastewater plant construction services, pre-agreed a tariff for transport, electricity and water services with the Ugandan government. Similarly, the Nam Theun 2 power station in Lao is funded via a power purchase agreement between the Electricity Generating

As-Samra Wastewater treatment plant PPP is a 25 year long BOOT contract signed between the Government of Jordan and the SPV As-Samra Wastewater Treatment Plant Company Limited. The Kalangala Infrastructure Services (KIS) project operates as a multi-donor BOOT PPP with KIS, the SPV, responsible for the investment and maintenance of infrastructure for 15 years. The Government of Uganda signed a memorandum of understanding with InfraCo, who set up and maintain a 54% equity stake in KIS, in 2006.

Authority of Thailand and Electricity de Lao, a state owned utility. In such cases, off-taker or counterparty risk is driven by the public sector's ability to honour contractual obligations.

Other business risks refer to market risk (also often referred to as demand risk) associated with a varying demand for the water-related services. The initial As-Samra wastewater treatment plant for example in Jordan had reached operational capacity. As a response, jointly with the Government of Jordan, the Millennium Challenge Corporation (MCC) expanded the plant as part of its compact with the country. However, it is anticipated that the expanded plant will reach full capacity shortly, and a third expansion was announced in December 2018 by the European Bank for Reconstruction and Development (EBRD) and the European Union (EBRD, 2018[4]).

In addition, such projects are often not without substantial macroeconomic risks. While not unique to the water sector, foreign currency risks often make the participation of private sector investors in infrastructure projects challenging. Infrastructure projects are often funded in local currencies. However, a large portion of infrastructure projects are still financed in US dollars, resulting in volatile debt servicing cash flow needs. Good examples of currency matching is the expansion of the As-Samra wastewater treatment plant as well as the Nam Theun 2 which involved substantial local currency debt financing (Naughton, DeSantis and Martoussevitch, 2017[1]).

The extent of political and regulatory risks are, by nature, context and project specific. However, in this subsector they tend to drive commercial investment decisions given the project attributes of large scale, long-term tenure and the decisive role of governments. Interventions in regulations affecting revenues such as changes in tariffs or taxation, but also political risk such as breach of contract are of major concern to private investors and hard to quantify *ex ante* (see also (World Bank/OECD, 2015[5])). Official development actors can contribute to addressing such systematic risks by providing political risk guarantees. The World Bank Group's guarantee arm MIGA, for instance, provided a total of USD 91 million in political risk insurance in 2005 to private investors in the Nam Theun 2 project (MIGA, 2006[6]).

Often, project valuation of large scale MPWI is complex and time-consuming due to their variety in value propositions. For example, the Nam Theun 2 Project in its entirety spanned over 30 years. During that time there was the Asian financial crisis in 1997 which had impacted the projects scope and size, with the planned budget for the project cut from USD 2 billion to USD 1.3 billion. Delays to the start of construction and cost overruns contributed to higher risk levels for the project. In addition, understanding and potentially mitigating environmental and social risks of MPWI infrastructure is associated with significant time commitments and costs for project development. For example, the design and preparation of the economic, environmental and social safeguards for Nam Theun 2 took over ten years to complete. In addition, the costs of mitigating negative social and environmental costs such as displaced persons can be significant – a total of USD 78.6 million was provided by the Nam Theun 2 Power Company for the environmental and social programme, equivalent to over 6% of total project costs. Brownfield investments, in contrast, can often more easily commercial private capital due to the lack of construction risk and available track record in both operations and financing.

Moving towards integrated landscape-based approaches may add a variety of characteristics and project attributes to those associated with discrete MPWI projects. For example, landscape-based approaches often leverage a business' or project's holistic exposure to a landscape into the project design (Kissinger et al., 2013[3]). These approaches can benefit downstream water users such as water supply companies, hydropower plants, irrigation districts, agricultural associations and other private sector actors such as food and beverage companies (TNC, 2011[7]). Beyond social and environmental impact, these approaches can deliver direct economic benefits to businesses and other water users within a specific spatial area, either by avoiding losses and/or by increasing profits. The rationale to invest in such landscape-based approaches is hence often driven by considerations of direct positive and/or avoided negative impact in the local context. For example, water supply companies and beverage companies benefit from improvements in water quality that result in reduced treatment costs, reducing operational risk, and are, as such, inclined to invest in projects addressing these areas. For example, the Monterrey Metropolitan Water Fund (FAMM) provides an example of corporate business funding of landscape-based approaches due to downstream benefits. Heineken, which has a brewery located in area, provided the majority of grant funding for the fund.

4.3. Blended finance instruments and mechanisms for financing multipurpose water infrastructure and landscape-based approaches

Blended finance models in this subsector apply a whole range of instruments and mechanisms to mobilise commercial finance in this subsector.

As in water and sanitation utilities and off-grid sanitation, *grants* and *technical assistance* are often needed in the early stages of project development. The Development Bank of Southern Africa (DBSA) is developing a project to fund large scale municipal water conservation, water demand management (WCWDM) and cost recovery programmes. The City of Tshwane currently loses millions of Rand annually as a result of water losses in the network and poor cost recovery. To address this, DBSA and the Infrastructure Investment Programme of South Africa (IIAPSA) are grant funding the pre-feasibility and feasibility studies of the planned WCWDM programme in the City of Tshwane, which will report identify, assess and mitigate technical, institutional, legal and financial risks.

The programme is still in its first phase and includes the design of a financing mechanism that is a combination of conventional debt financing with structured finance characteristics. The aim is to enable the city to borrow the money required to conduct infrastructure improvements for the WCWDM programme while strengthening its balance sheet over the implementation of the programme by using the proceeds to invest in projects that lead to savings through reducing water losses. The savings and improved levels of cost recovery out of the sub-projects implemented will allow the Metro to finance future sub-projects through a combination of debt and own funds as well as grants. As the programme is rolled out, less debt will be required to finance the new sub-projects as the city will be able to fund a larger portion through own funds generated from the savings and improved revenues (Figure 4.1.).

Figure 4.1. DBSA Programme outline for the City of Twshane

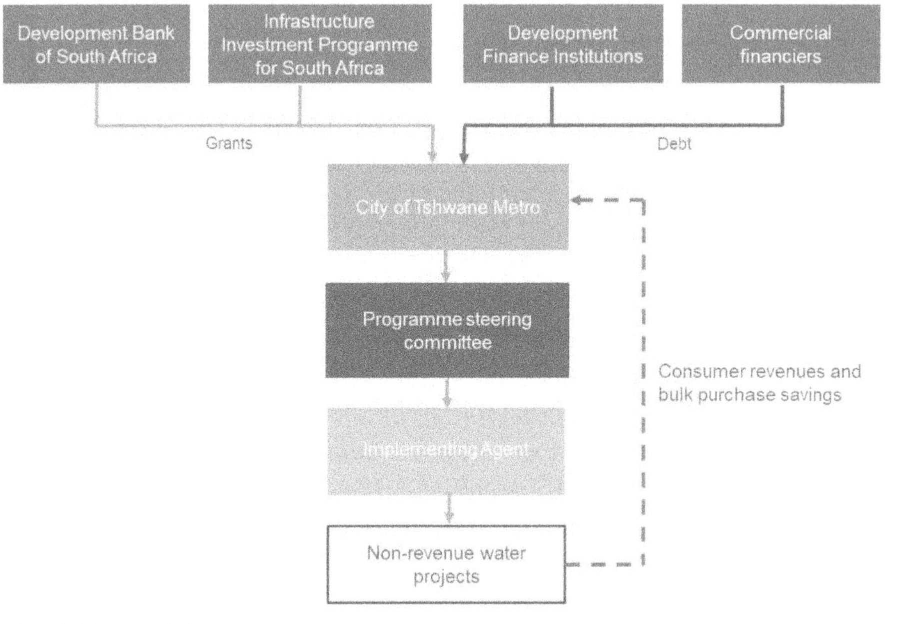

Source: Undisclosed project documentation.

Grants play not only a key role in project development but also in the financing structure which helps to enhance the credit profile of projects that have a social and economic benefit. For the expansion of the As-Samra wastewater treatment plant the viability gap grant funding of USD 93 million from MCC and a USD 20 million grant from the Jordanian government were critical to leveraging an additional USD 110 million from the private financiers for the project.

Strategic direct investments in projects finance vehicles via *loans* or *equity* can be an effective tool to mobilise private capital. This was the case with Nam Theun 2. Total project volume of the SPV Nam Theun 2 is more that USD 1 300 million of which 85% is commercially financed. The complexity is reflected in the total of 27 institutions including MDBs, DFIs, Export Credit Agencies (ECAs) and Thai Banks involved. The SPV Nam Theun 2 Power Company is owned by Lao Holding State Enterprise (LHSE), a state-run business, which helped to mobilise USD 327.5 million of private investments in equity. The LHSE has in turn raised a combination of debt (e.g. AFD, EIB and ADB) and grant funding (AFD, World Bank's IDA). Debt is raised in both LCY by local banks and USD by international lenders, which overall reduces the currency volatility risk for the project company. Also, this large-scale project received grant funding and technical assistance for project development from the World Bank.

Figure 4.2. A simplified Nam Theun 2 financing scheme

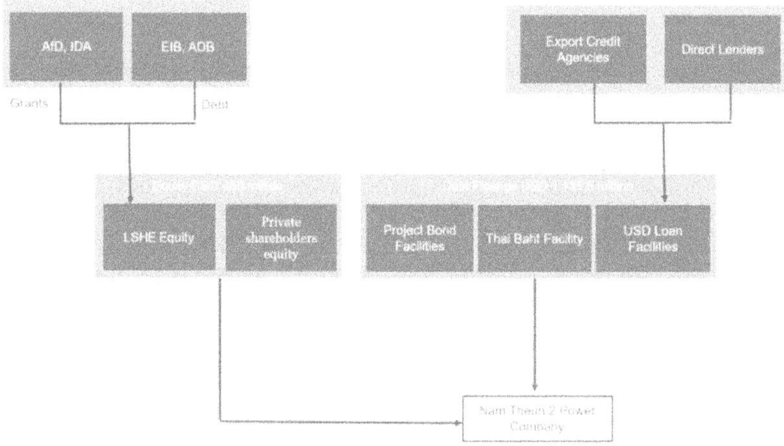

Source: Authors based on (Naughton, DeSantis and Martoussevitch, 2017[1]).

Syndicated loans are an effective way to mobilise private finance by reducing transaction costs and building on the track record of the arranger's expertise in the particular area. For example, the expansion of the As-Samra Wastewater treatment plant, the sponsor Suez raised syndicated debt financing, whereby the Arab bank as lead arranger mobilised further debt from Jordanian local financial institutions. The USD 110 million syndicated loan is Jordanian dinar-denominated and has a tenor for 13 years with the option to extend to 20 years. This is the longest maturity that had been obtained for a Jordanian dinar-denominated loan by 2012. While the interest rate during the three-year construction period for the treatment plant expansion has been fixed, following the commissioning of the plant, the loan evolved to a floating rate linked to the average prime lending rate of four local banks.

Guarantees are in general a very effective tool in blended finance. The instrument is currently not utilised at scale in the water and sanitation sector (GuarantCo, 2018[8]). For example, GuarantCo provides a joint partial credit risk guarantee with USAID of USD 1.8 million to Nedbank as part of the financing for the Kalangala Infrastructure project, covering the non-payment of debt service. In addition, MIGA provided USD 91 million in political risk insurance for Nam Theun 2 Power Project (MIGA, 2006[6]). The guarantee of USD 86 million covers a loan by Fortis Bank NV against risks of war and civil disturbance, expropriation, breach of contract, transfer restriction and inconvertibility.

Landscape-based approaches enhance MPWI projects in respect to various dimensions, as described before. Innovative financing approaches are aiming to monetise and share economic, social and environmental returns related to investments in the landscape.

The Water Funds model, first set up by The Nature Conservancy (TNC) and the Municipality of Quito, brings different types of public and private actors together in *pooling mechanisms* that provide long-term, sustainable finance to contribute to water security and sustainable watershed management through nature-based solutions. The Inter-American Development Bank (IADB), in partnership with TNC, FEMSA Foundation and the Global Environment Facility (GEF), launched the Latin American Water Funds Partnership in 2011. The partnership creates and strengthens Water Funds across the region. Water funds, as such, are blended *collective investment vehicles* which pool grant funding from donors, households and commercial sector actors. At the same time, water funds offer no direct financial return to investors. Any returns generated by the funds are reinvested into watershed management and conservation activities. These include, for example (see Figure 4.3):

- Payment for environmental services, including watershed management and biodiversity conservation,
- Water resources management as part of sustainable land use programs,
- Conservation projects to protect the natural habitats where these services originate, and
- Adaptation measures to mitigate negative impacts on water resources due to climate change.

While contributions to the water funds do not generate financial returns to investors, the benefits of more effective watershed management can attract non-repayable capital contributions from large commercial water users such as water supply companies, hydropower plants, irrigation districts, agricultural associations and other private sector investors such as breweries and soft drink companies.

Large water supply companies for instance can benefit as improvements in water quality result in reduced treatment costs. This can lead to savings that exceed conservation investments, with a reduction in annual expenses for filters, chemicals to purify and potentially removing the need to develop treatment plants. Similarly, investments in nature-based solutions in watersheds can reduce the recurring costs for hydropower plants reducing sediment accumulation and silting of dams. Water Funds have proven to be a replicable model with 24 funds created so far in Latin America.

Figure 4.3. The Water Fund Endowment Model

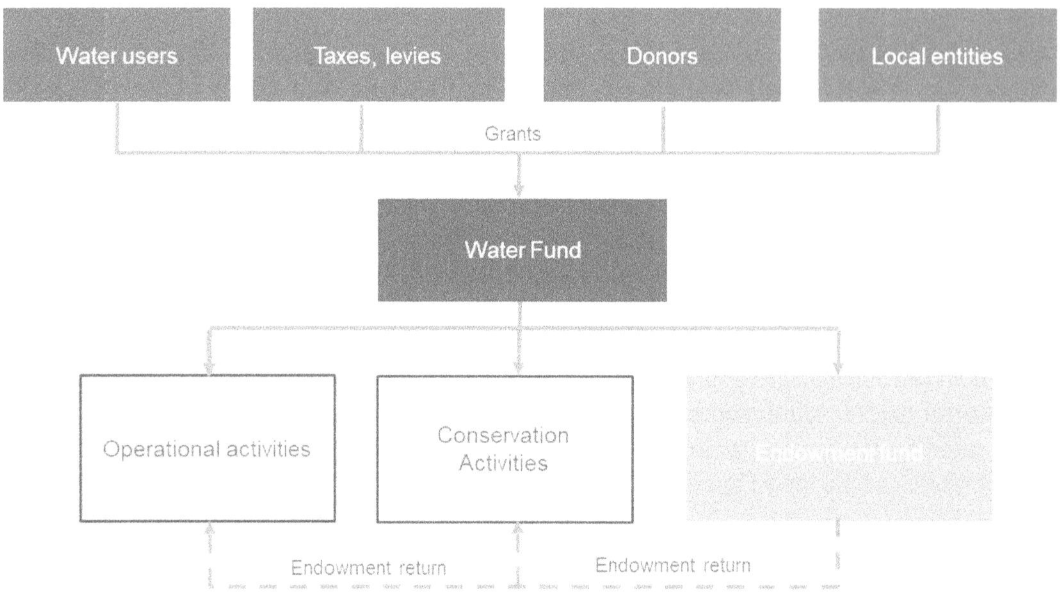

Source: (TNC, 2011[7]).

The Monterrey Metropolitan Water Fund (FAMM) in Mexico for example is predominantly funded by commercial actors. It has been set up in 2013 in order to increase the water security in the city of Monterrey located on the banks of the Santa Catarina River. Over 60% of the water used in the metropolitan areas come from Cumbres de Monterrey National Park, located within the San Juan River basin. In the basin soil erosion and the loss of vegetation cover have negatively impacted run off control. In addition, changes in land use and forest have also contributed to the degradation of the water supply to Monterrey metropolitan area. The region is also prone to hurricanes which can have further devastating effects on the city. To respond to these challenges, the FAMM invests in reforestation, restoration and soil management to improve water infiltration in the San Juan River basin and reduce the potential impact of natural disasters. FAMM has more than 40 partners including the federal government, the local government, businesses and NGOs. Over 75% of the grant funding is provided by the private sector, with the remainder of funding provided by bilateral and multilateral development agencies. Heineken, who operate a brewery within the region, funds and sits on the board of FAMM.

Water Funds show how both the need for tailor-made solutions in developing and financing landscape-based approaches as well as a large degree of replicability of the funding model can be aligned. Beyond anchor investments in the funds, development actors have a crucial role to play in providing *technical assistance and grant funding* to develop innovative solutions in the first place. Despite successes to date, quantifying, monetising and linking the benefits from increased water security to the beneficiaries who can take the investor role as well as attracting external investors remains an important challenge in financing landscape-based approaches.

In the same vein, landscape-based approaches can also incorporate discrete MPWI projects. The Songwe River Basin Development Programme (SRBDP) is currently being developed by the governments of Tanzania and Malawi. It consists of the implementation of a 10-year programme with integrated industrial irrigation, water supply, and hydropower schemes which jointly aim to enhance food and energy security for the basin communities in the context of the overall socio-economic development of Malawi and Tanzania. Under the SRBDP, water supply projects for small towns around Kasumulu (Tanzania) and Songwe (Malawi) will be implemented, tapping water from the Lower Songwe dam reservoir after producing hydropower (180.2MW). The Irrigation and Drainage scheme participants will be required to pay a fee for water provided from the new dam through the canals being planned. In collaboration with the Climate Resilient Infrastructure Development Facility (CRIDF), the Africa-EU Water Partnership Programme (AEWPP) being implemented by the Stockholm International Water Institute (SIWI) is supporting the Songwe River Basin Commission (SRBC) to mobilise commercial financing for the SRBDP. SIWI is working with the SRBDP to develop a commercially sound business model for the agri-businesses that will underpin the irrigation schemes along the Songwe River, while CRIDF supports the project preparation of the water supply to Kasumulu and Songwe. To improve the financial viability of the project, a blended finance approach is planned that will involve significant concessional debt from development actors, equity from the two Governments of Malawi and Tanzania, as well as commercial debt and equity from private investors.

In order to attract more commercial capital to improve water security via landscape-based approaches, WWF have launched the Bankable Water Solutions Initiative in partnership with DFIs and private sector firms. The initiative seeks to catalyse a stream of bankable projects that will improve water management and offer acceptable financial returns to investors. An example of partnership and project currently being scoped is the Kafue River basin in Zambia. WWF has partnered with the Zambian government, private sector firms, and the Dutch DFI FMO to tackle several interlinked challenges facing the basin, which are critical for the Zambian economy. The Kafue Flats provide a promising case for piloting bankable project, because of the inter-related risks of water supply, increase in hydropower and expansion of agriculture in the basin. Through WWF's Bankable Water Solutions Initiative, a landscape finance plan is being developed with a pipeline of projects that aim to develop water resources with a positive net impact in the Kafue Flats Landscape. WWF has secured seed funding to execute a pre-feasibility study for an industrial wastewater treatment plant as the first step in assessing the bankability of such a project. The project has also attracted funding from a private sector investor, AB InBev, which have a direct interest in the supply system risks/reliability for Lusaka of their own operations and their customers' wellbeing, as well as the sugar supply chain.

Similar to MPWI projects, financing landscape-based approaches is challenging in both developed and emerging economies, with additional layers of complexities in the latter group. At the same time, it can be relevant for future project development to understand the mechanics behind recent approaches that attract commercial investment at scale into such projects. An example that provides such an illustration derives from the Waikato region in New Zealand. This innovative financing approach provides insights into how a venture-capital like hybrid debt instrument exercising both debt and equity characteristics is applied in order to improve agricultural land use and convert conventional dairy farms to organic (Box 4.1). This example demonstrates how commercial actors can be mobilised into a portfolio of projects building on a blended model where a government-related authority provides credit enhancement. However, the project itself is early stage. It remains to be assessed whether this model could be replicated in developing countries.

Box 4.1. Blended finance in the Waikato Region, New Zealand

The Waikato region produces greenhouse gas emissions that are 50% higher per capita than the New Zealand average. In 2016, the Waikato River Authority and the Waikato Regional Council commissioned an impact investment feasibility study. As a result, the dairy sector has been prioritised given the cash flow generation opportunity through conversion of conventional to organic dairy in comparison to afforestation.

The Waikato River Limited was created to increase sustainable agricultural land use. That is, the SPV plans to use proceeds from a bond issuance to acquire conventional farms and convert them to organic farms with measures to mitigate negative environmental effects such as afforestation and riparian tree planting by waterways. The feasibility study has indicated that by targeting land use change and low input farming, a significant cumulative reduction of environmental externalities can be achieved. In addition, the now organic farms are expected to increase their turnover by producing organics milk, which can achieve a higher price in the market than conventional milk.

The company will issue a hybrid NZD 100 million bond with a tenor of ten years with an annual coupon payment. At the same time, the asset-backed hybrid bond includes a swap, and as such exhibit both fixed income and equity characteristics. This will allow investors to generate explicit financial returns, i.e. interest payments, as well as partake in the implicit gains via the equity ownership. Indeed, within the ten year to maturity, the farm land is expected to appreciate in value. This profit will be shared between bond investors, the government related organisation and the SPV manager. The government acts as a guarantor in mobilising commercial bond holders as any shortfall in coupon payments will be guaranteed by a governmental organisation.

Figure 4.4. The blended structure of the hybrid bond

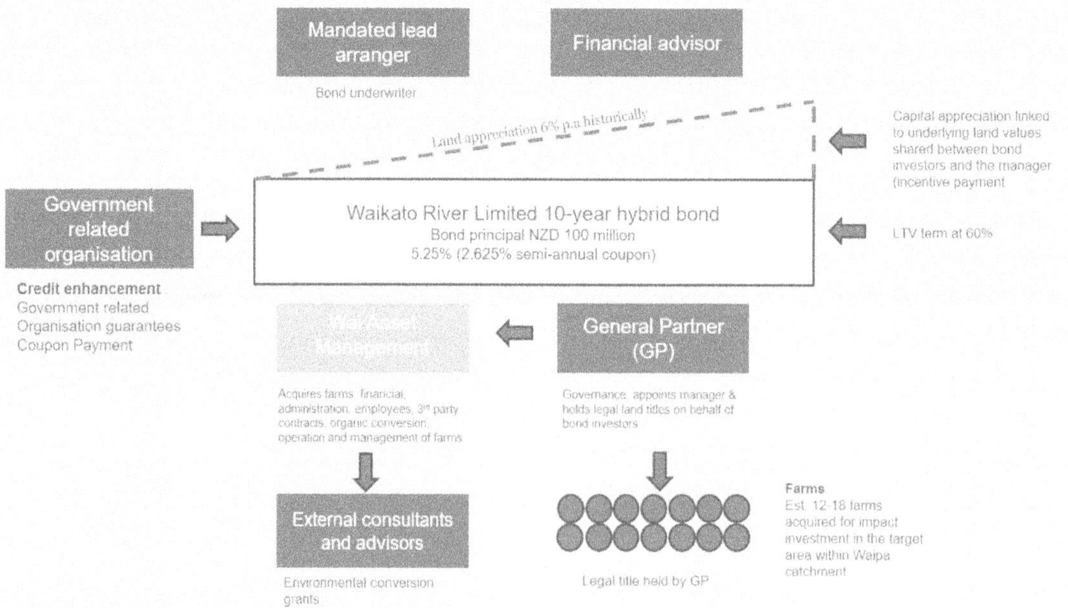

Source: Information Memorandum, Waikato River Authority, 2018 (Waikato River Authority, 2018[9])

4.4. A typology of investors in multipurpose infrastructure and landscape-based approaches

MPWI projects have the potential to mobilise *commercial finance* from banks and institutional investors as they present a familiar business case for such type of investors. Particularly large scale projects with clear revenue streams such hydropower or largescale wastewater treatment plants can attract financing from institutional investors. For example, the range of private actors such as Standard Chartered, BNP Paribas and ING involved in financing the Nam Theun 2 power plant. Local and regional banks have an important role to play in financing and providing technical assistance for projects. In addition to fostering local ownership, local currency financing fosters actively the financial sustainability of infrastructure projects that are funded in local currency through their revenue streams. Local financing in Thai Baht was a key part of the financing approach for Nam Theun 2, for example.

However, it is more challenging to mobilise commercial investment into landscape-based approaches. Local private sector companies are already engaging in the provision of grant capital to watershed management projects that deliver positive benefits the spatial area they are operating in. For example, water funds often attract private capital from downstream water users as brewers or soft drink companies operating within the region. Heineken's financing of the FAMM Water Fund is an example.

MDBs and DFIs are an important player in blended finance models for financing infrastructure, including MPWI. They engage typically in providing (senior) debt financing or guarantees, but also act as equity sponsors. Proparco, the French DFI for example, classifies water-related projects under their mandate to support infrastructure. The organisation invests primarily into countries in Sub-Saharan Africa and the Mediterranean, and largely funds projects in the financial and power sectors, 36% and 22% respectively, followed by "other infrastructure," 12%, of which water projects would be included (EDFI, 2018[10]).

Increasingly MDBs and DFIs are mainstreaming nature-based solutions into their operations. For example, the IADB based on their experience with the Latin American Water Funds Partnership, have worked in identifying a potential pipeline to mainstream nature-based solutions into specific IADB loans. As a result, a USD 250 million loan in design phase in Panama and in a USD 200 million loan in execution phase in Pernambuco, Brazil were identified. Both operations are expected to co-design and develop green and grey infrastructure for the conservation of the Juan Diaz watershed (Panama), and the Ipojuca watershed (Brazil). In addition, the EIB Water Sector Lending Policy published in December 2017 set out the importance of landscape-based approaches to integrated water resource management (EIB, 2017[11]). From 2012-17 the World Bank Group financed 81 projects that employed green infrastructure/nature based solutions of which approximately 18 were in the water and sanitation sector (Browder et al., 2019[12]). Historically, the World Bank has treated grey infrastructure and environmental projects as separate, however, as evidence base for the benefits of integrating nature-based solutions into infrastructure projects, the bank has increasingly looked at financing and promoting green-grey infrastructure approaches (Browder et al., 2019[12]).

Importantly, *development actors* as DBSA and the Dutch government (though FMO) engage actively in the development of projects, which may serve as a stepping stone to mobilise commercial investment. *NGOs* are also active in project development. WWF provided technical expertise and grant funding for feasibility studies for planned projects in the Kafue River Basin as well as launching the Bankable Projects Initiative for landscape-based solutions. In developing Water Funds, TNC provided technical assistance, watershed management expertise as well as promoting nature-based solutions and the Water Funds mechanism more broadly.

4.5. An assessment of the sustainable development impact

Large-scale infrastructure projects should include an assessment of potential negative environmental and social impacts during the project preparation stage, design and implementation. Programmes should be implemented to mitigate these risks and progress consistently monitored. While this requires additional resources it is essential to ensure that potentially negative effects such as displaced persons, ecosystem and wild life damage and potential threats to water quality are identified and addressed. The experience of Nam Theun 2 has shown that a co-ordinated approach can help mitigate negative impacts if it is strongly integrated into project planning and financing. Most explicitly, the project is a key part of the government's poverty reduction strategy with an agreement in place between the World Bank and the government that revenues generated from the project would be invested in poverty reduction and public services (World Bank, 2018[13]). However, the additionality of revenues as result of revenues as opposed to previously planned budget increases was not verified. This was in part due to the lack of baseline data and changes in budget classification (World Bank, 2018[13]). Therefore it is unknown whether revenues replaced planned government expenditure increases. Efforts have been made to increase transparency with revenue statements shared with the World Bank and State Audit Office as well as audits of projects funded by revenues (World Bank, 2018[13]). The breakdown of the disbursement of the services for the project can be found below.

Table 4.2. Disbursement of Nam Theun 2 (NT2) Revenues

Sector	Million USD	Percentage
Education	65.81	35.3
Health	62.14	33.3
Public Works and Transport	15.67	8.4
Energy, Mining and Agriculture	24.32	13.1
Natural Resources and Environment	1.31	0.7
Poverty Reduction Fund	9.91	5.3
Projects Implemented by Provinces	7.05	3.9
Total	186.22	100

Source: State Audit Organization (SAO) Audit Reports 2009/10 - 2015/16, MoF Data FY15/16 and FY17 & World Bank 2018, Implementation Completion and Results Report – Nam Theun 2 (World Bank, 2018[13])

The 2017 assessment following the closure of the environmental and social programme concluded that the environmental targets around watershed management, water quality and species protection had been met (World Bank, 2018[13]). The report found that 100% of displaced persons had been resettled and 97% villages met income targets - the rural poverty line which was approximately double pre-project incomes. The remaining 3 % received additional in-kind support. In addition 100 000 people lived downstream and were potentially vulnerable to the project induced changes. A programme to compensate for lost land and provide infrastructure and livelihood training, and a fund to provide investments for livelihoods was created by the World Bank. However, the complexity, large scale, long lifetime and the variety of actors involved undermine a comprehensive and causal assessment of the full negative or positive impacts upon downstream users (World Bank, 2018[13]).

The expansion As-Samra Wastewater Treatment plant has provided the capacity for the Government to treat 70% of the countries' wastewater and provided 133 million cubic meters of treated water per year for irrigation in the Jordan Valley. In addition, the As-Samra plant has improved the long-term sludge management and disposal practices further helping to preserve Jordan's water resources. At the end of the Compact between the Government and MCC approximately 375 000 households or 2 023 000 individuals had benefitted from additional supplies of freshwater as larger volumes wastewater agricultural use in the Jordan Valley. Approximately 8 500 households in the Jordan Valley or 46 000 individuals now receive a consistent supply of high-quality treated wastewater that can be used for irrigation (MCC, 2018[14]). The As-Samra plant also provides bio-solids for potential reuse in fertilizer and fuel, and produces 80% of its own energy needs, from biogas and hydropower. However, unanticipated population growth means that the plant is already nearing full capacity despite initial projections that it would serve Jordan's water needs until 2025. As a result, in December 2018 the EU and the EBRD announced their intention to expand the plant further increasing the capacity of the plant from 365 000 kilolitre per day (kl/day) to 465 000 kl/day (EBRD, 2018[15]).

The Mwena water treatment plant has a capacity of over 400 kl/day and the reservoir tanks/storage facilities of 200 kl. The improvement has enabled Kalangala Infrastructure Services to supply water to Bugala Island 24 hours. As a result of safe water supply services, the population on Bugala Island has experienced a reduction in medical expenses due to reduction water in borne diseases and improved sanitation. Those villages now supplied with clean, safe water have seen an 80% drop in waterborne disease. However, other aspects of the programme have increased costs for residents in the area with the ferry service developed as part of the project now charging a fee for use whereas it had previously been free.

Landscape-based approaches aim at developing approaches that are embedded in local communities from the project development phase. As such, the local community can benefit from better management of watershed and greater water security but also environmental conservation. Improved land management and agricultural practices can have large positive impacts on downstream users. In total, the Latin American Water Funds Partnership implemented by the IADB led to the implementation of watershed conservation projects that have benefitted over 70 million people downstream from 2011-16. In addition, 1 675 667 hectares of natural habitat has been conserved or positively impacted by Water Fund operations (The Latin American Water Funds Partnership, 2018[16]).

4.6. Subsector-specific insights

For MPWI, blended finance models are an established financing instrument for typically large-scale special purpose companies directed to delivering multiple water-related benefits.

- MPWI is typically financed via project companies that are run as SPVs and hence constitute a well-known structure to commercial investors. Commercial finance can be mobilised in MPWI projects with a predictable revenue proposal. This can include for example MPWI projects that incorporate an energy element such as hydropower which is associated with tariffs or PPAs that cater to the financial sustainability of a project.
- Within MPWI projects, development actors engage in providing equity and debt, underwrite guarantees to mitigate risk for commercial financiers, or provide viability gap grant funding with ambition to mobilise commercial financing typically from local and international financial institutions; sponsor equity is often sourced from private or public utility companies.
- In addition, technical assistance for project development is an effective enabling blended finance instrument. Large-scale MPWI projects have long preparation and financing tenors, which leaves them vulnerable to changing circumstances. Assessing and addressing negative environmental and social impacts of large scale MPWI should be integrated from the outset.

For landscape-based approaches, blended finance can potentially operate as a fit-for-purpose financing instrument as it brings together different stakeholders responding to their individual investment preferences.

- Development financiers are gaining experience with landscape-based approaches which can mobilise local actors with a stake in improved water resources management. Moreover, nature-based solutions are also attracting increasing interest, as a complement to conventional grey infrastructure to deliver multiple water-related benefits.

- Technical assistance and pooling mechanisms are prevalent blending instruments in landscape-based approaches, which have mainly attracted public funds and corporate philanthropy to date, rather than commercial finance. The use of blended finance remains at an early stage. A functioning model thus far has been to source grant funding from commercial actors.
- Landscape-based approaches need models and innovative approaches to materialise often implicit revenue streams such land and other asset appreciation (see Figure 4.5). For example, Water Funds build on the implicit gains for locally-based actors (e.g. water utilities and corporates) who benefit from avoided costs due to improved watershed management in the spatial area. It remains a challenge to externalise such avoided costs in a way that commercial investment can be attracted.

Figure 4.5. An investor perspective on return sources in landscape-based approaches

Source: Authors.

References

Browder, G. et al. (2019), *Integrating Green and Gray: Creating Next Generation Infrastructure*, https://wriorg.s3.amazonaws.com/s3fs-public/integrating-green-gray_0.pdf?_ga=2.83621790.901310088.1557143599-562307893.1557143599 (accessed on 6 May 2019). [12]

EBRD (2018), *EBRD and EU to support expansion of As Samra wastewater treatment plant in Jordan*, https://www.ebrd.com/news/2018/ebrd-and-eu-to-support-expansion-of-as-samra-wastewater-treatment-plant-in-jordan-.html (accessed on 20 March 2019). [15]

EBRD (2018), *EBRD and EU to support expansion of As Samra wastewater treatment plant in Jordan*, https://www.ebrd.com/news/2018/ebrd-and-eu-to-support-expansion-of-as-samra-wastewater-treatment-plant-in-jordan-.html (accessed on 25 April 2019). [4]

EDFI (2018), *Meet our members: Proparco*, https://www.edfi.eu/member/proparco/ (accessed on 12 September 2018). [10]

EIB (2017), *EIB water sector lending orientation: strengthening water security*, https://www.eib.org/attachments/strategies/eib_water_sector_lending_orientation_en.pdf (accessed on 6 May 2019). [11]

GuarantCo (2018), *GuarantCo - Portfolio - Kalangala Infrastructure Services*, https://guarantco.com/portfolio/kalangala-infrastructure-services/ (accessed on 25 April 2019). [8]

Kissinger, G. et al. (2013), *Reducing Risk: Landscape Approaches to Sustainable Sourcing*, https://static1.squarespace.com/static/58d6cc1e17bffcffb801edde/t/594bb41c9de4bbeab83d9b32/1498133592619/landscapes-for-people-food-and-nature.pdf (accessed on 25 April 2019). [3]

MCC (2018), *Jordan Compact | Millennium Challenge Corporation*, https://www.mcc.gov/where-we-work/program/jordan-compact (accessed on 25 April 2019). [14]

MIGA (2006), *Hyrdopower in Asia: The Nam Theun 2 Project*, http://www.miga.org (accessed on 25 April 2019). [6]

Naughton, M., N. DeSantis and A. Martoussevitch (2017), "Managing multi-purpose water infrastructure: A review of international experience", *OECD Environment Working Papers*, No. 115, OECD Publishing, Paris, https://dx.doi.org/10.1787/bbb40768-en. [1]

OECD (2008), *Public-Private Partnerships: In Pursuit of Risk Sharing and Value for Money*, OECD Publishing, Paris, https://dx.doi.org/10.1787/9789264046733-en. [17]

The Latin American Water Funds Partnership (2018), *IMPACTS - Fondos de Agua*, http://waterfunds.org/esp/impacts/ (accessed on 25 April 2019). [16]

TNC (2018), *Water Funds: Field Guide 2018*, https://www.tncmx.org/agua/wp-content/uploads/Files/Agua/Water-Funds-Field-Guide-2018.pdf (accessed on 14 August 2019). [2]

TNC (2011), *Water Funds Conserving green infrastructure: A guide for design, creation and operation*, https://waterfundstoolbox.org/ (accessed on 25 April 2019). [7]

Waikato River Authority (2018), *Information Memorandum NZ$100M Hybrid Bond Impact Investment*, https://waikatoriver.org.nz/wp-content/uploads/2019/04/Waipa-Investment-Memorandum-April20191.pdf (accessed on 29 July 2019). [9]

World Bank (2018), *Implementation Completion and Results Report: Nam Theun 2 Social and Evironment Project*, http://documents.worldbank.org/curated/en/134811549388324604/pdf/p049290-icr-01302019-636846554068325875.pdf (accessed on 25 April 2019). [13]

World Bank/OECD (2015), *RISK AND RETURN CHARACTERISTICS OF INFRASTRUCTURE INVESTMENT IN LOW INCOME COUNTRIES*, http://www.g20india.gov.in/pdfs/F- (accessed on 14 June 2019). [5]

Annex A. Primer on blended finance

A primer on blended finance for water and sanitation

Blended finance in the development co-operation landscape

In order to respond to the global development challenges, the 2015 Addis Ababa Action Agenda (AAAA) put emphasis on the need to work closer with and increase investments of the private sector. Blended finance offers a promising approach to crowd-in additional commercial finance that is not currently invested for development outcomes, whereby blended finance is defined as the strategic use of development finance for the mobilisation of additional finance towards sustainable development in developing countries (OECD, 2018[1]). Development finance can thereby be concessional finance or non-concessional finance coming from public or private sources, e.g. philanthropic actors. Additional finance focuses on commercial finance, which refers to finance invested at commercial rates from private sources or public investors such as sovereign wealth funds.

The OECD Development Assistance Committee (DAC) Blended Finance Principles for Unlocking Commercial Finance for the Sustainable Development Goals are a regulatory framework that work towards sustainability of blended finance as a one approach to mobilise private finance in donors' toolboxes (Figure A A.1). The OECD is currently developing guidance complementing the principles to provide further evidence to DAC members. Moreover, the OECD conducts a series of deep-dives into blended finance in specific contexts, including by sectors (water and sanitation with this publication; agriculture forthcoming in 2020), income group (OECD/UNCDF, 2019[2]) and a contribution to UNCDF (2018[3]), as well as geographical contexts as fragile contexts (Basile and Neunuebel, n.d.[4]).

At the same time, blended finance is a multi-stakeholder concept, strongly dependent on concerted efforts by development actors, commercial players and civil society. The Tri Hita Karana (THK) Roadmap was launched to establish a shared value system among international partners including governments such as Indonesia, Canada or Sweden, Multilateral Development Banks (MDBs) and Development Finance Institutions (DFIs), the private sector as well as civil society organisations (CSOs) and think tanks. Under the THK Roadmap, these actors engage in co-ordinated action to ensure that blended finance is contributing to sustainable development, including on developing good practice. This publication adds to the ambitions of the THK Roadmap by shedding light on blended finance in the water and sanitation sector.

Figure A A.1. OECD DAC Blended Finance Principles

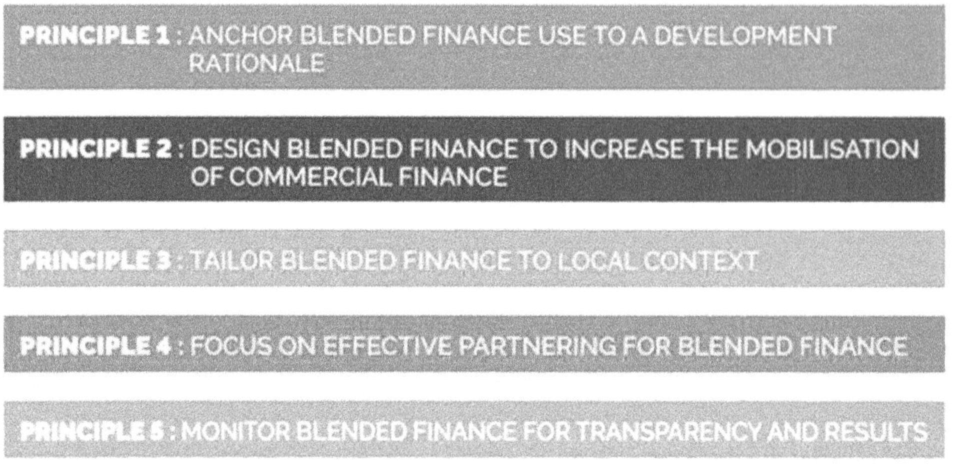

Source: (OECD, 2017[5]).

Blended finance instruments and mechanisms

Blended finance approaches can be categorised according to mechanisms and instruments. Blended instruments include equity, debt or mezzanine investments directly invested in typically companies or projects (OECD, 2018[1]). By deploying development finance in either of these forms, commercial investors can be mobilised by improving the viability of a transaction or enhancing its credit profile. Blended finance transactions can involve direct monetary contributions without expectation of repayment and non-monetary provisions in the form of advice or assistance, i.e. grants and technical assistance respectively that further strengthen project capacity to help mobilise commercial investment.

Instruments also include credit enhancement in the form of insurance and guarantees, which can cover for example credit risk (typically partially) or political risk. Guarantees back commercial financier's confidence by transferring the risk of for instance debt service shortfall to the guarantor against a fee.

Figure A A.2. Blended finance instruments and mechanisms

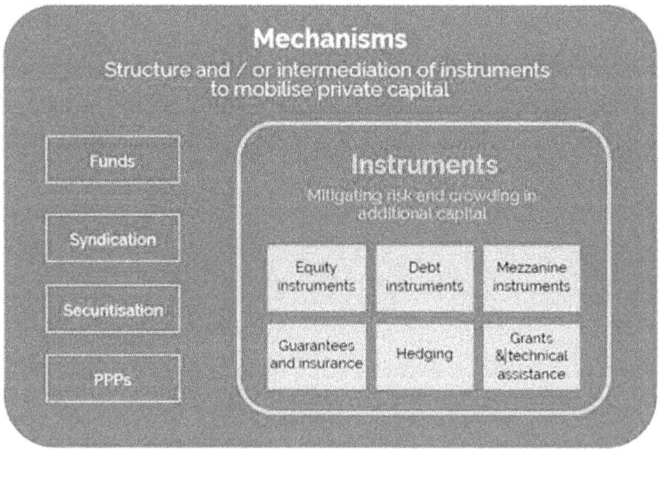

Note: PPP = Public-Private Partnerships
Source: (OECD, 2017[5]).

Investment funds or collective investment vehicles (CIVs) constitute mechanisms to address issues related to high risk, small investment volumes and limited sectoral or regional financial knowledge. In doing so, investment vehicles provide access to a portfolio of projects specific sectors or regions using different type of instruments, including equity, debt or guarantees. Thereby, larger volumes of commercial investment can be channelled towards sustainable development projects. Commercial investors benefit from risk diversification as well as often first loss coverage provided by development actors in the case of structured funds.

Syndicated loans are an efficient way to reduce transaction costs, while harnessing the due diligence capacity of the lead arranger, typically MDBs in blended structures. Commercial lenders disburse additional credit volumes as part of the syndicated loan. PPPs can be financed in blended forms, for example when development actors are mitigate credit or political risk for commercial actors.

Annex B. Case Studies: Water and Sanitation Utilities

The Kigali Bulk Water Supply project: When a Public Private Partnership meets Blended Finance

Development finance

The International Finance Corporation (IFC)'s Public-Private Infrastructure Advisory Facility (PPIAF), a multi-donor trust fund, provided technical assistance and capacity building to Rwanda's Energy Water and Sanitation Authority (EWSA) leading up to the project. Following the decision to split EWSA into two specialised water and energy utilities in 2014, PPIAF developed a high-level strategy for the operation of WASAC, Rwanda's Water and Sanitation Corporation. PPIAF also provided capacity building training to government officials to support the water sector reform process.

Three organisations affiliated to the Private Infrastructure Development Group (PIDG) helped finance the project at different stages of its development:

- DevCo, a facility managed by the IFC and funded by PIDG, provided initial financial support and technical assistance to the government of Rwanda to cover the legal, financial, technical and environmental feasibility assessments of the project.
- The Emerging Africa Infrastructure Fund[1] (EAIF) provided USD 19 million in senior debt and USD 2.6 million in junior debt. The EAIF also crowded in African Development Bank funds amounting to USD 19 million in junior debt.
- PIDG's Technical Assistance Facility provided a USD 6.25 million grant to cover upfront capital costs and avoided an increase in water tariffs as a result of the project.

Commercial finance

The private investor in charge of implementing the public-private partnership was competitively selected by the IFC via a bid order. The United Arab Emirates-based Metito consortium, comprising Metito Utilities Ltd. and Metito Overseas Ltd. (hereafter, Metito), won the 27-year concession to build, operate and maintain and transfer the facility. Metito, one of the world's largest water utility providers, provided USD 11 million in equity finance.

Challenge

The Government of Rwanda has committed to achieving universal and reliable access to safe drinking-quality water supply to Kigali and to the country's 12.4 million inhabitants, as set out in its Vision 2020 strategy.

There is a lack of access to piped water supply in Rwanda, with only 40% of the total population connected to a supply system as of 2015. There are also significant inequalities between urban and rural areas; 73%

of the population have access to a piped water supply connection in urban areas, whereas only 27% of the population in rural areas has such access (WHO/UNICEF, 2019[6]).

Rapid urbanisation and population growth in Kigali, the capital city of Rwanda, are straining the city's infrastructure services. The limited public water production and supply capacity, impaired by a high rate of non-revenue water, frequently leads to water rationing for increasing numbers of water supply subscribers in the city.

Solution

The Kigali Bulk Surface Water Supply project (Figure A B.1) is the first large scale water treatment facility financed through a public private partnership model in Sub-Saharan Africa (excluding South Africa), and one of the first water infrastructure projects established through a Build Operate and Transfer arrangement. The 27-year public-private partnership agreement, which includes a 2-year grace period for project development and construction and 25 years of operation and maintenance, benefits from a guarantee from the Ministry of Infrastructure of Rwanda. The agreement is funded via a tiered capital structure, which means that Kigali Water Limited (KWL), a fully owned subsidiary of Dubai-based Metito, will build, maintain, and operate the treatment plant and sell drinking quality water to WASAC, Rwanda's public water utility in charge of the transmission and distribution and sole off-taker of the project. At the end of the 27 years period, Metito will transfer KWL over to WASAC, which will maintain and operate KWL.

The EAIF, itself a blended finance fund, is the mandated lead arranger of the financing. EAIF provided USD 19 million in senior debt and USD 2.6 million in junior debt to KWL, and crowded in an additional loan of USD 19 million from the African Development Bank, covering USD 40 million in debt facilities with 18-year tenors out of the total project capital investment of USD 60.9 million. A USD 6.25 million technical assistance grant was provided by PIDG's Technical Assistance Facility (TAF) to cover the viability gap, reduce up-front costs, and allow the government to increase the number of households connected to the piped water supply system without raising tariffs. The USD 11 million remaining balance was provided by Metito as equity finance. DevCo supported and advised the Government of Rwanda in assessing the feasibility of the project and in determining the most suitable public-private partnership structure in line with the development objectives of the Rwandan government.

Figure A B.1. The Kigali Bulk Water Supply financing structure

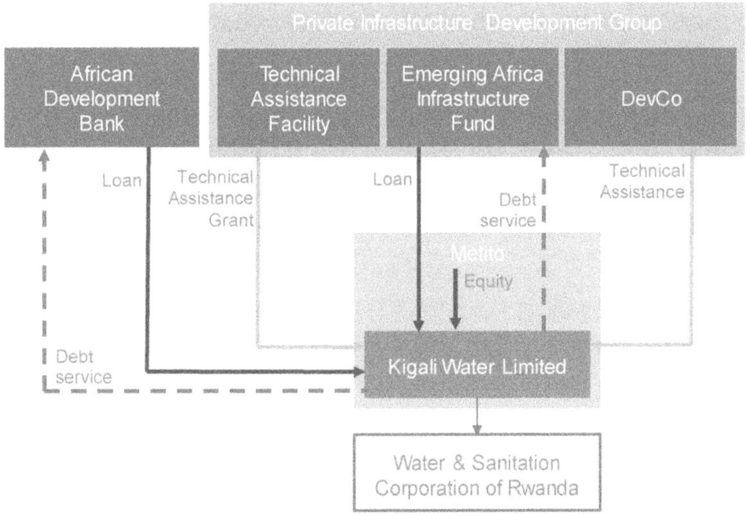

Source: Authors.

The discrepancy between the currency of the loans and equity (USD), and the local currency with which revenue is generated (Rwandan francs, RWF), can have implications for the overall cost and level of risk of the project. The blended package was denominated in US dollars, a hard currency that both matched construction costs (also in USD), and allowed for cheaper debt than would be locally available due to concessional rates and/or longer maturities. However, foreign financing also entails a higher level of currency risk. As the revenue generated from the utility will be in RWF, a free floating currency, foreign investors can incur losses in the event of currency fluctuations (e.g. local currency depreciation). In the case of the Kigali project, currency negotiations led to significant delays. From a government perspective, the ultimate risk is that costs resulting from currency depreciation could be passed on to customers. Concessional development interventions, such as the provision of guarantees, can play a role in mitigating this risk while increasing the investor's confidence that profits will remain stable in the event of currency depreciation.

In the case of the Kigali Bulk Water Supply project, some of this risk was addressed by minimising project costs and maximising efficiencies with the decision to separate the distribution infrastructure from the plant under a distinct concessional loan. On top of the contribution of wells, a water treatment plant, and two pumping stations, the project initially included the transmission and distribution infrastructure necessary to maximise the impact of the project - three reservoirs, distribution pipelines, and a pumping station. However, it was subsequently agreed that greater efficiency could be achieved by allocating that infrastructure to the municipal utility, WASAC, under a separate arrangement with funding from the Government of Rwanda and the African Development Bank. This enabled each of the water production and distribution projects to independently find the most suitable financing solutions and maximise their impact on operational efficiency and benefits to end users, and to reduce the overall cost of the project from USD 79 million to USD 61 million.

In many developing countries, maintaining water and sanitation tariff affordability is necessary to ensure access for all. In fact, as part of the negotiation process, Rwanda's regulators did not support a proposed increase in the water and sanitation tariffs (which was later abandoned). Further investigation, which resulted in delays in the implementation of the project, highlighted that the currency risk was not the only cost-raising factor. The break-down of the water tariff revealed that high electricity costs and taxes were significantly raising costs. As these are set by the Government of Rwanda, they were beyond the control of Metito and the lenders. In a public private partnership arrangement, it is recommended that the private sector be transparent towards the Government, regulators, and the national water utility about the composition of the tariff in order to avoid "hidden" profits. Increased transparency not only raises the confidence of all stakeholders, it can also shed light on hidden costs.

Expected impact

Upon completion of the project, which is still on-going, the resulting infrastructure is expected to produce and supply 40 mega-litres of clean, drinking quality water every day to over half a million Rwandans (40% of Kigali's water supply needs).

Jamaica's Credit Enhancement Facility: Establishing innovative financing mechanisms for the sustainable financing of wastewater management

Development Finance

In this project, development finance came from Global Environment Facility (GEF)-funded Caribbean Regional Fund for Wastewater Management project (CReW), an innovative approach that aimed at reducing the negative impacts of untreated wastewater on the environment and human health in the Wider Caribbean Region. The USD 20 million fund was dedicated to the implementation of innovative financing in wastewater management in 13 countries (Antigua and Barbuda, Barbados, Belize, Costa Rica, Jamaica, Guatemala, Guyana, Honduras, Panama, Saint Lucia, Saint Vincent and the Grenadines, Suriname, and Trinidad and Tobago) between 2011 and January 2017. The fund aimed at addressing three challenges: i) bridging the funding gap for investments in wastewater collection and treatment; ii) supporting reforms in legislative, regulatory, and policy frameworks to facilitate greater investment in wastewater management; and iii) foster peer learning among key stakeholders in the Wider Caribbean Region. The Inter-American Development Bank and United Nations Environment Programme jointly managed the implementation of the CReW project along five components: (1) Investment & Sustainable Financing; (2) Reforms for Wastewater Management; (3) Communication, Outreach & Training; (4) Monitoring & Evaluation; (5) Project Management.

Commercial Finance

Commercial finance came from the National Commercial Bank, which disbursed a loan to the National Water Commission (NWC), the largest provider of potable water and wastewater services in Jamaica.

Challenge

Wastewater management has been a significant challenge for countries in the wider Caribbean region. Water supply is often prioritised at the expense of wastewater management infrastructure in this frequently water-stressed region. On the one hand, governments in the region have traditionally not put into place funding mechanisms, including tariffs, sufficient to develop, operate, and maintain adequate wastewater collection and treatment systems. This leads to difficulty in accessing financing, such as commercial loans, for investments in the sector. On the other hand, with the exception of Jamaica, which has applied wastewater tariffs to recover the operation and maintenance costs of its facilities, attempting cost-recovery through customer charges would significantly increase tariffs to a level that may pose affordability issues. Combined with a lack of financing, this resulted in insufficient investment. As of 2011, 85% of wastewater discharge in the Caribbean Sea remained untreated, over half of the population in the region lacked connection to a sewer system, and only 17% was connected to an adequate wastewater collection and treatment system. Before the implementation of the Jamaican Credit Enhancement Facility (JCEF), 80% of Jamaica's population had access to piped water in 2010, whereas just about 18% had a sewer connection, and little over 7% of effluent sewer was treated (WHO/UNICEF, 2019[6]),

Governments recognise that land-based sources of pollution from domestic, industrial and agricultural uses have significant negative impacts on marine resources, putting economic development and human health and well-being at risk. In Jamaica, the government of took steps in addressing wastewater treatment issues. From 1995 to 2010, 5 wastewater treatment plant were built. In 2013, the government passed the wastewater and sludge regulation, to ensure that effluent waters are adequately treated, to make it mandatory to connect new developments to NWC's sewer system and to support the National Environment and Planning Agency in taking enforcement action against non-compliant wastewater operators and developers. Further demonstrating its commitment to reducing pollution from untreated wastewater, Jamaica ratified the Cartagena Convention[2] and the Protocol Concerning Pollution from Land-Based Sources and Activities (hereafter, the LBS protocol) in 2015. By the time the country ratified the Convention and Protocol, national wastewater treatment standards stemming from the 2013 regulation were more stringent than the LBS protocol standards (UNEP, 2015[7]).

Nevertheless, although regulations supported better performance, a significant proportion of the country's wastewater facilities kept on operating below required standards. The NWC, a statutory organisation tasked with providing water and wastewater services island-wide, operates more than 70% of the country's sewage treatment facilities, with small private and community-based water and sewerage providers servicing the rest of the market. Prior to the JCEF project, 44 of the NWC's 70 wastewater facilities were in need of rehabilitation to meet national effluent standards, and a significant proportion of them had been in operation for over twenty-five years, outliving their estimated economic lifespan and experiencing declines in operational efficiency. At the same time, the NWC had been experiencing high rates of non-revenue water due to leakage and illegal connections. In 2013, non-revenue water was estimated at nearly 70% of all water produced that year. There was thus a need to invest in the rehabilitation of deteriorating infrastructure.

Adequate long-term financing, particularly with tenor exceeding ten years commensurate with the long-lived capital investment required, is rarely available from commercial banks in Jamaica. To address the lack of financing, in 2008, the Office of Utilities Regulation of Jamaica allowed for NWC's tariffs to include the K-Factor programme, a pre-determined surcharge collected monthly from customers. The K-Factor revenues capitalise a special account earmarked for priority water and wastewater investment projects. In the initial phase, it was envisioned that NWC would secure loans for selected projects against the expected K-Factor cash inflows and the inflows used to repay these loans. This model was not fully operational and a hybrid format was implemented (loans as well as direct payments were taken from the monthly deemed amount). Despite the gap, efficiency improvements resulting from these investments have been reflected as an X-Factor amount (a "give back" to the customers for the efficiency gains derived from the use of the K-Factor funds) on the customers' bills. The X-Factor is set by the Office of Utilities Regulations and this amount has fluctuated from around 5% (from 2009 to 2013) down to 0% in 2014, and up to 6.2% in 2018. Despite these efforts, the NWC continued to face difficulty in accessing the capital needed to expand and upgrade its water and wastewater services.

Solution

The CReW was an innovative approach to provide financing for investments to reduce the negative impacts of untreated wastewater on the environment and human health in the wider Caribbean region. The Global Environment Facility developed the CReW to address three significant challenges: i) strengthen the enabling environment by supporting policy and legal reforms; ii) increase access to financing; and iii) raise the priority placed on wastewater treatment. As part of its initial phase of implementation - *Investment and Sustainable Financing*, the CReW project selected four countries in which to implement Pilot Financial Mechanisms: revolving funds in Belize, Guyana and Trinidad and Tobago, and a credit enhancement facility in Jamaica. The objective of these locally defined pilot projects was to determine innovative financing strategies that could then be applied to other CReW participating countries.

To support local commercial bank financing of wastewater project, the CReW fund selected Jamaica's proposal to create a credit enhancement facility. Following approval from the Ministry of Finance, the NWC established the Jamaica Credit Enhancement Facility (JCEF) in October 2012 as a USD 3 million guaranteed fund, which was placed in a reserve account at the National Commercial Bank of Jamaica in January 2013 (Figure A B.2). In August 2015, the NWC signed a loan agreement with the bank to obtain commercial funding from local financial institutions of the local currency equivalent to USD 12 million (JMD 1.4 billion[3]) for a period of at least 12 years. With a 4:1 leverage of financial resources, the JCEF allowed for the fund capitalised by the USD 3 million CReW grant to provide secondary collateral against loans disbursed to the NWC. The initial collateral and source of payment for the loan came from annual K-Factor revenue. This instrument reduced the default risk initially associated with the borrower (NWC) and allowed greater access to commercial capital through the provision of a steady revenue stream earmarked for investments in priority wastewater and water supply projects. The total amount of K-factor revenue that is needed to service the debt is approximately JMD 51 billion, with an average yearly amount of JMD 4.1 billion.

Figure A B.2. The Jamaica Credit Enhancement Facility financing structure

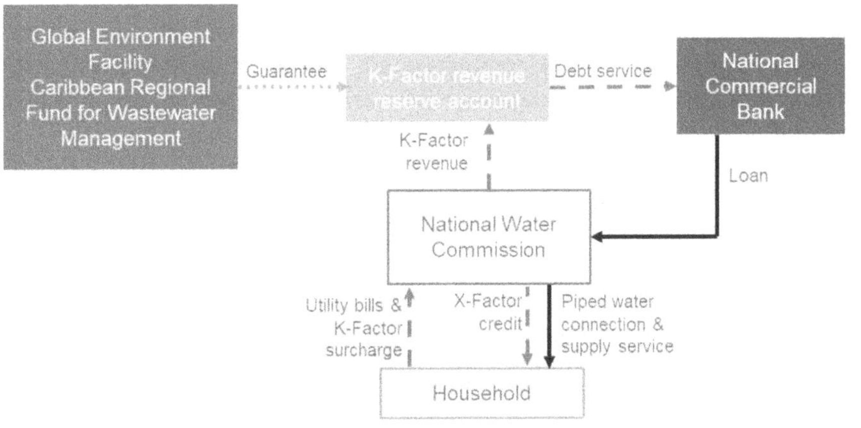

Source: Authors.

Impact

Of the 44 wastewater facilities to be upgraded by K-Factor funds prior to the JCEF, 13 were initially selected to be rehabilitated or replaced under the CReW project to meet national effluent compliance standards. One reason for the initial selection of a subset of projects was to ensure that the loan reflected only a portion of the K-Factor, such that K-Factor revenues were approximately 60% higher than annual debt servicing for the loan. This over-collateralisation of the loan reduced the credit risk, an important step to build local banks' confidence as the JCEF was a fist-time structure in Jamaica. These 13 facilities were regrouped in four packages. However, three challenges contributed to increasing costs constrained the CReW to reduce the number of packages down to three. First, a lack of co-ordination among stakeholders on the JCEF's objectives and planning, and lengthy negotiations over the currency of the loan to minimise foreign exchange risk caused the loan agreement to be signed 34 months after the establishment of the JCEF. Second, there were significant delays in the procurement process, partly because of the issuance of an inadequate tender (design and build rather than rehabilitate) in an attempt to speed up the process. Finally, the project's timing collided with Jamaica's required servicing of international debt, leading to a lack of fiscal space to uphold project obligations.

A total of eight facilities were eventually selected to participate in the CReW's initial phase of implementation through the JCEF: i) two wastewater treatment plants were rebuilt; ii) three plants were set to be decommissioned and connected to the central sewer system through the design and construction of new conveyance systems; and iii) three plants were set to be rehabilitated. These plants follow national effluent standards and the CReW mandate enabled for more effective wastewater management and for greater financial sustainability of the NWC, contributing to reducing the contamination water bodies and risks to public health.

The first package (replacement of two wastewater treatment plants) was completed by December 2016 and handed over to the NWC for operation. The work undertaken as part of the second package (design and construction of three conveyance systems and decommissioning of three wastewater treatment plants) was estimated to be 94% complete as of June 2019. The third package (rehabilitation of three wastewater treatment plants) is also nearing completion, estimated at 87% completed as of June 2019.

In 2018, the NWC secured a bond of JMD 15 billion, of which JMD 12.5 billion was guaranteed by the K-Factor funds. The capital raised will be used to settle K-Factor related loans as well as to finance other capital / K-Factor projects that were previously approved by the Office of Utilities Regulations. Additional financial support has been provided from the bond to facilitate shortfalls in the second and third packages' work contracts as a result of unforeseen increases in material and labour costs.

Moving forward, Jamaica is working to build on lessons learned from the JCEF to further develop and upgrade the water and sanitation infrastructure. The NWC still experiences high systemic inefficiencies, with an estimated 49% of all water produced lost to leakage and theft. Of the initial 44 facilities targeted, there remains at least 25 in need to be decommissioned, rebuilt, rehabilitated or constructed. Several wastewater treatment plants are being packaged for bid invitations and are proposed to be financed by the recently acquired bond.

Blended finance solutions to expand utilities' services in Indonesia

Development finance

Water.org, a non-governmental organisation funded by philanthropic donations, partnered with the Batang District Water Supply Company Indonesian, an Indonesian regional water supply company located in Central Java, Indonesia, in 2016 to support the expansion of urban utility water and sanitation services. Regional companies, or Perusahaan Daerah Air Minum (PDAMs) in the Bahasa language, are mandated to provide clean water and are monitored by their respective regional government. Water.org also partnered with the microfinance institution (MFI) Koperasi Mitra Dhuafa (KOMIDA) from late 2018.

Commercial finance

KOMIDA provides debt as microfinance loans to low-income households seeking a connection to a piped water supply or a sanitation system.

Challenge

The Batang District is located in Central Java Province and consists of 15 sub-districts ("Kecamatan") comprising 248 villages with a total population just over 700 000, of which 16% is urban and 84% is rural. The PDAM serves nearly 42% of Batang District's population and is driven by its mission to, among other things, increase service coverage and provide clean water supply services to the community. To achieve these goals, the PDAM faced the dual challenge of attracting the commercial finance needed to expand its services into poorer areas, and adapting their array of services to better attract and retain poorer clients, which have a distinct set of financial needs.

Solution

Batang District PDAM partnered with Water.org in September 2016 with a special focus on growing the number of low-income clients it served.

One component of achieving that goal was client-facing: not only offering a wider range of financing options that catered to the needs of low-income households, but also alerting potential clients to these newly-available financing options through targeted advertising efforts. Batang District PDAM was already offering some financial services in-house to its clients – a system in which the up-front connection cost is paid over a series of instalments that are incorporated into a water client's monthly utility bill – but sought Water.org's technical assistance to increase its efficiency in this activity and also advertise its availability. Additional finance options for PDAM clients who are existing clients of KOMIDA are available through the MFI's dedicated water and sanitation loans. This provides KOMIDA clients with a greater variety of financial options from which they can connect to Batang District PDAM services. Additional technical assistance on market analysis and demand generation was also provided to the PDAM.

The second component of serving more low-income clients required expanding pipelines and services to more areas where this population lived. Batang District PDAM again sought technical assistance from Water.org, which came in the form of assistance in the development of Standard Operating Procedures for financial service offerings, financial recordkeeping and reporting, and human resources recruitment. Having these procedures in place positioned the PDAM as more attractive to investors when applying for the credit they needed to expand. Figure A B.3 illustrates the financing structure.

Figure A B.3. The Water.org – PDAM – KOMIDA financing structure

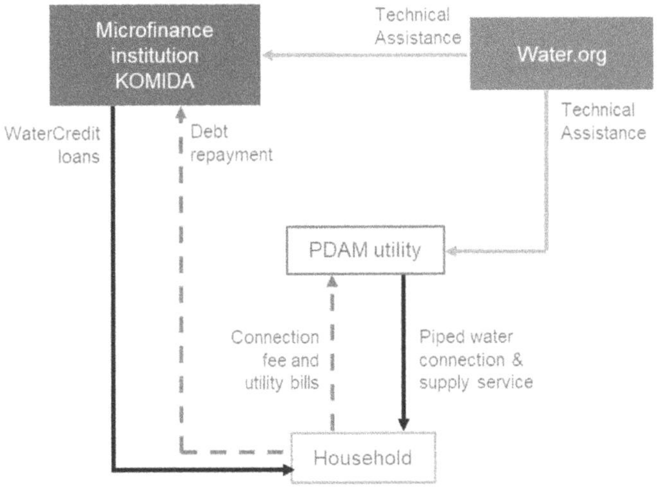

Source: Authors.

Impact

As of August 2018, nearly 5 000 new households were connected to the Batang District water supply system. Notably, 1 650 of those households (approximately 34%) benefitted from internal financing options provided by the PDAM, while the majority of others were able to self-finance the connection. Batang District PDAM increased their clients utilising internal PDAM financing from approximately 70 per month in 2015–16 to 248 in June 2017.

In addition to this new client acquisition, Water.org's assistance in preparing a detailed engineering design report helped the PDAM secure approximately USD 50 000 in grant funding from the Indonesian government to extend their pipeline in 2018, enabling them to serve an additional 5 000 households. The goal over the final year of their formal partnership is to secure commercial finance to continue extending the distribution network and scale in-house financing.

To summarise, the PDAM utilised concessional support from Water.org to build its client base. A few of those new clients financed their connections via loans available through Water.org interventions with MFIs, but many are financing through the PDAM itself or through their own means. Simultaneously, the PDAM also improved its internal processes to successfully apply for public grant support. Those fundamental improvements also serve to assist Batang District PDAM in eventually being successful at attracting commercial investment.

Blended finance solutions to support rural Filipino utility service expansion

Development finance

The Municipal Development Fund Office of the Philippines Department of Finance, Provincial Government of Palawan, provided the Nara Water utility; Water.org partnered with the utility to increase the number of customers connected to the network and extend its paying customer base.

Commercial finance

Water.org partnered with the following microfinance institutions to extend their portfolio to offer microloans earmarked for water and sanitation projects: ASA Philippines, Negros Women for Tomorrow Foundation; Taytay sa Kauswagan, Inc.; Community Economic Ventures Inc.

Challenge

Narra Water - a newly-constituted municipal economic enterprise for Narra Municipality, Palawan Province, the Philippines, and owned by the Narra Local Government Unit, took a 20-year loan valued at USD 2.46 million with 6% interest per annum in 2015. The purpose of the loan was to build out the Narra Water Supply System to cover the 23 villages of the municipality, a significant expansion beyond the three villages (approximately 1 400 households) that were being served at the time. The loan was provided on concessional terms by the Municipal Development Fund Office, which manages the second-generation funds from foreign-assisted projects (Narra Water would not have qualified for a loan from a commercial bank). Construction of new facilities began immediately, but active recruitment of new paying customers for the services was not prioritised.

In 2017, Narra Water realised that rapid client acquisition was needed to generate the revenues required for meeting the instalment payments on the loan. The company faced the challenge of repaying their concessional loan with revenues generated from a potential client base that not only needed to be convinced to connect to the network, but also might face challenges paying for that connection.

Solution

Water.org collaborated with Narra Water starting in September 2017 along two fronts. First, it worked with the utility to improve its capacity in customer acquisition. This included mapping the community to understand where new potential clients were located and developing outreach strategies for these prospective customers. Water.org also provided technical assistance to the utility staff on financial management. This included analysis to determine that a monthly revenue of one million Philippine Pesos (approximately USD 18 460) per month was required in order to cover the loan instalments while they were still in the grace period of the loan. This revenue could be achieved only when 4 300 households were connected and paying water tariffs.

On the second front, Water.org involved its existing WaterCredit partner, the microfinance institution ASA Philippines, in the Narra opportunity. As a WaterCredit partner, ASA Philippines offers water and sanitation loans to low-income borrowers. It sources the capital it lends locally but receives technical assistance from Water.org in developing and marketing viable water and sanitation loan products. Approved clients receive the water and/or sanitation loan and repay it at market rates. Over time, three other microfinance institutions offering WaterCredit loans also became involved: Negros Women for Tomorrow Foundation, Taytay sa Kauswagan, Inc. and Community Economic Ventures Inc.

Making a connection between a utility actively working to expand its business and a lender looking for clients interested in taking a loan to finance the cost of connecting to the local water utility benefits the utility, the lender, and the clients, who now have access to a reliable source of drinking water. Figure A B.4 illustrates the Narra Water financing approach.

Figure A B.4. The Water.org - Narra Water financing structure

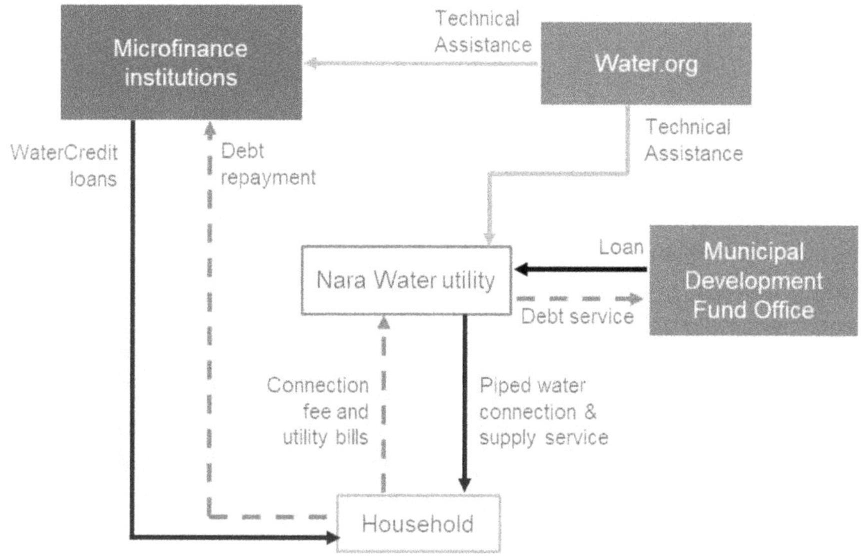

Source: Authors.

Impact

Before the alliance with Water.org in September 2017, Narra Water was serving approximately 2 000 households. After one year of collaboration, 1 500 new households were connected to the system. Approximately 9% of the new connections were realised through microloans to low-income households, and those who did not take loans for the connection fee paid for it directly, mobilising more than USD 15 000 of revenue from low-income households. As a result, Narra Water's revenue has increased by 138%. Expansion efforts brought the utility much closer to the 4 300 households needed to cover operating expenses and make debt service payments during the grace period, and to reach the total of 6 000 connected households needed ensure timely payment of principal and interest dues by 2020. The Provincial Governor has been so encouraged by the speed at which Narra Water has been connecting new households to municipal water services that in August 2018, he called for this model to be replicated across all towns with water projects in the Palawan Province.

This case study highlights the at times complex intertwining of actors and approaches that blended finance solutions can take to create positive outcomes. Narra Water received a concessionary loan from the Department of Finance, for which it requires revenue from its clients to repay. Assistance identifying those potential clients and marketing to them came through Water.org at no cost to Narra Water, and a portion of the new clients had the finances available to connect due to a loan provided from local microfinance institutions, which are offering this loan as a result of its participation in the WaterCredit initiative. While ASA Philippines received technical assistance and a small project preparation grant from Water.org to develop the water and sanitation loan product, the loans disbursed to aspiring Narra Water clients were sourced through local Filipino banks, and the Narra Water customers pay their water tariffs and (where applicable) loan instalments from their private funds.

Thus, blending can happen at multiple levels. It likely would have been preferable for the utility to develop a plan for repaying its debt in advance before taking a loan for infrastructure expansion. A blended finance approach could have been adopted in the design and early implementation stages, which could have avoided the scenario. Nevertheless, even at a later stage Water.org and Narra found avenues for bringing in private financing at a later stage to extend and improve services and to enable the utility to get back on track with its debt obligations, and the technical assistance they provided helps ensure that Narra Water will have such financial plans in place before taking another loan.

The Philippine Water Revolving Fund: bridging the rural-urban divide in access to water utility services

Development finance

The Japan International Cooperation Agency (JICA)[4] provided a concessional loan to the Development Bank of the Philippines (DBP) through the Environmental Development Project. Through this project, an innovative pooled financing mechanism called Philippine Water Revolving Fund (PWRF) was established. JICA's concessional loan to the DBP was backed by a sovereign guarantee from the Government of the Philippines Department of Finance. The PWRF is a co-financing facility designed to encourage private sector participation in water and sanitation financing as well as make such financing affordable through blended finance. An initial financing mix of 75%-25% between JICA/DBP funds and participating commercial finance institutions, respectively, was adopted under PWRF, which also has a revolving feature for the ODA component ensures sustainability.

Commercial finance

To encourage the participation of commercial financiers, participating private banks benefit from a partial guarantee from the Local Government Unit Guarantee Corporation (LGUGC) which is backed by a co-guarantee from the United States Agency for International Development's (USAID) Development Credit Authority.

Challenges

The Philippines made progress in increasing the proportion of people with basic access to water, from 86% in 2000 to 91% in 2015 (WHO/UNICEF, 2019[6]). However, the country remained behind other countries in the Southeast Asian region, including Thailand (98%), Malaysia (96%) and Vietnam (92%) in terms of access to piped water supply. Basic access to sanitation has also improved, from 67% in 2000 to 75% in 2015 nationally. Nevertheless, about a fifth of all municipalities had less than 50% water supply service coverage, and there was a decline in the rate of access to piped water nationwide from 47% in 2000 to 43% in 2015 (WHO/UNICEF, 2019[6]).

There is a lack of information on the total number of water service providers in the country. However, based on survey commissioned by the World Bank in 2015 through the National Water Resources Board, water districts and local government units make up 3% and 17% of the total water supply service providers of the country, respectively. The majority of water service providers is managed by small-scale water and sanitation associations, co-operatives, or unnamed providers (66%) or other sources (15%) that offer only point source water service.

In terms of credit availability, private banks, while endowed with sufficient liquidity, lack experience in lending to water service providers, thus offer short tenors (7 to 10 years) and are reluctant to lend to the water and sanitation sector. The financial environment when the PWRF was conceptualised was also characterised by high market-driven variable interest rates (9-12% per annum). Moreover, some water districts and local government units' inability to meet loan requirements further contributed to lack of investments in the sector.

Solution

The PWRF (Figure A B.5) was created to provide water service providers access to private finance through the blending of ODA funds channelled through the DBP with commercial finance from private banks. The PWRF was implemented alongside two market-enabling components: a credit rating system to inform investors and a water project appraisal training to lenders with little prior experience lending to the sector.

Figure A B.5. The Philippine Water Revolving Fund financing structure

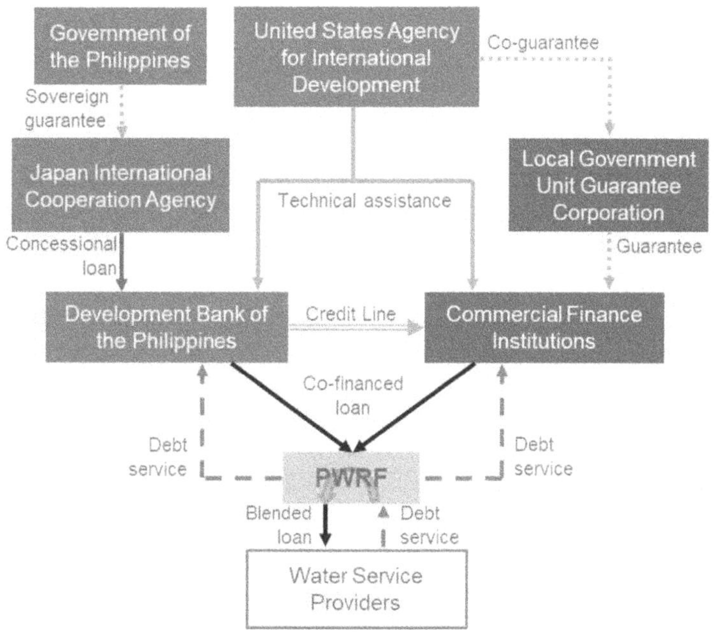

Source: Authors.

The PWRF is an innovative financing facility developed in consultation with the Government of the Philippines to improve access to financing in the water and sanitation sector. The PWRF was implemented in the context of co-operation efforts between the USAID and JICA. This was triggered by the US-Japan Clean Water for People Initiative launched in 2002 to support the Millennium Development Goals on water and sanitation targets. Henceforth, extensive consultations were held among the Government, USAID and JICA supported by studies commissioned by both development partners to establish the viability of the PWRF and develop its framework.

At the same time, policy reforms were being implemented in the water and sanitation sector, including Republic Act 9275, which supports the implementation of the Clean Water Act and Executive Order 279, which required a shift of financing of creditworthy utilities to market and cost-based lending from banks. In 2004, a pilot PWRF account was implemented to identify strengths and weaknesses in the conceptual approach, forming a basis for the final design and implementation of the PWRF. In particular, the pilot highlighted the need for PWRF to: i) provide affordable loans at fixed, below market interest rates and longer tenors (15-20 years); ii) incentivise all stakeholders for loans to be arranged by a single entity rather than multiple parties; and iii) for the project to be aligned with public policy goals and support both refinancing and new investments.

In September 2008, JICA and DBP signed a loan agreement where the PWRF financing window was incorporated. With its blended financing element, other key features of the PWRF include:

- a liquidity risk cover is provided to local banks through a stand-by credit line from DBP and the Municipal Development Fund Office with a take-out feature offered to borrowers who cannot afford the bank's short tenor. Loans are disbursed on 7-year tenors, and are retired at the end of the period if the cash flow can support the repayment schedule. If not, whilst the 7-year tenor is maintained, the principal will be amortised over 20 years. The local bank will have an option to extend the maturity beyond 7 years, but if they choose not to, it can opt to be taken out by the either the DBP or the Municipal Development Fund Office or one of those entities can assume the loan and pay the local bank a balloon payment of the outstanding balance[5]. These loans become effective the day the local bank's loan expires and the balloon payment is triggered. With the stand-by credit line, local banks agree to amortise the loans over a 20-year period with a balloon payment by the end of the 7th year, and to exercise the option to renew the loan for another 7 years under the same terms and conditions. The stand-by credit line thus allows for a lower amortisation schedule for the water utility loan and provides an opportunity to test local banks' willingness to apply longer tenor on their loans;

- a credit risk guarantee providing partial guarantee from the LGUGC, a private entity, covering a maximum of 85% of commercial banks' exposure against a 1% guarantee fee, backed (up to 50% of the LGUGC's exposure) by a co-guarantee through the USAID-Development Credit Authority. The LGUGC guarantee provides credit risk enhancement to commercial banks thus reducing their credit risk exposure;
- a revolving feature, through a ring-fenced revolving account capitalised by principal repayments of borrowers on the ODA loan component to ensure sustainability of fund managed by the DBP.

Initially, JPY 1.5 billion (USD 13.4 million) was allocated by JICA to finance the PWRF window with concessional terms of 30-year maturity (inclusive of a 10-year grace period) at a fixed interest rate of 1.4% per annum.[6] The initial loan (from JICA to DBP) subsequently increased to JPY 7.6 billion (USD 67.8 million), and was fully disbursed by the end of the project in January 2017. By that time, the PWRF had financed 17 sub-projects totalling PhP 3.3 billion (nearly USD 65.5 million).

Impact

The PWRF was conducive to the expansion of utility services in the Philippines, and engaged private financial institutions in the provision of loans to water service providers. The sub-projects financed through PWRF resulted in an estimated 216 872 new household connections to water services as of January 2017. Financing terms of local banks have also improved, with tenors increasing from 7 years to between 15 and 20 years at lower, fixed interest rates.

Facilitating Access to Finance for water and sanitation infrastructure in Cambodia through blending solutions at multiple entry points

Development Finance

The French Development Agency (AFD) set up a concessional credit line with the Foreign Trade Bank (FTB) alongside a partial risk-sharing guarantee (ARIZ). The AFD also managed grant funding from the European Union (EU) to provide two kinds of technical assistance. The first one was dedicated to support the FTB structuration and knowledge on water and electricity infrastructure services. The second one was focused on small-scale private water operators aiming to develop a viable local intermediary ecosystem providing business brokering, engineering assistance and capacity building services. Part of the grant was also used to finance output-based subsidies to extend water and electricity services provided by small-scale private operators in small towns of Cambodia. To initiate the program, the World Bank Water Sanitation Program pre-funded the business plan preparation and engineering technical assistance in support of 20 small-scale private operators.

Commercial Finance

The Foreign Trade Bank (FTB) is a local commercial bank that was willing to diversify its portfolio by offering loans adjusted to the needs of water and electricity service providers.

Challenge

Access to piped water supply is lower in Cambodia than in most Southeast Asian countries, with a national average of 21% of the population having access to piped water supply in 2015 (Figure A B.6). There are significant inequalities in terms of both access and type of water provider between urban and rural areas, with 72% and 8% of the population having access to piped water supply respectively in 2015. Public utilities tend to serve large urban areas, including the capital Phnom Penh, while small-scale private water operators tend to serve rural areas. Remarkably, over the past two decades, a large amount of small-scale private operators have invested "spontaneously" in unstructured water supply and electricity utilities. The Cambodian case is relatively unique considering the number of small enterprises involved, the level of financial investments, their demonstrated initiatives and the financial risks taken. There are an estimated 300-400 small-scale water operators in the country, who rely on a full cost recovery system without access to public financing. The main factor preventing these private operators from upgrading and expanding their services is a lack of access to commercial financing. In Cambodia, water service providers tend to be business entrepreneurs with experience in finance and business management and little technical knowledge of the sector, which results in low quality infrastructure, and a low asset value. Moreover, the quality of infrastructure planning, design, financing and the capacity to prepare business plans are rather low. Additionally, when lending to the water sector, banks in Cambodia often do not conduct feasibility studies that account for economic and technical considerations of the projects, but instead consider the perceived capacity of the borrower to repay. Commercial banks also still consider water supply and electricity businesses to be risky. As a result, the few local and regional banks that lend to private water operators request: i) prohibitive collateral requirements, with values sometimes exceeding 200% of the loan, in the form of land and buildings; ii) high interest rates (from 8% to 15%); and iii) short tenors (up to 5 years) with no grace period. Furthermore, small-scale private operators do not have a clear incentive to deliver efficient levels of investment due to a very fragmented market; nor do they have incentives to deliver high quality water for that reason. This often leads to poor performance and further restricts their access to financing.

Figure A B.6. Access to piped water supply, Southeast Asia, 2015

Percentage of the total, urban and rural population of Southeast Asian countries with access to piped water supply

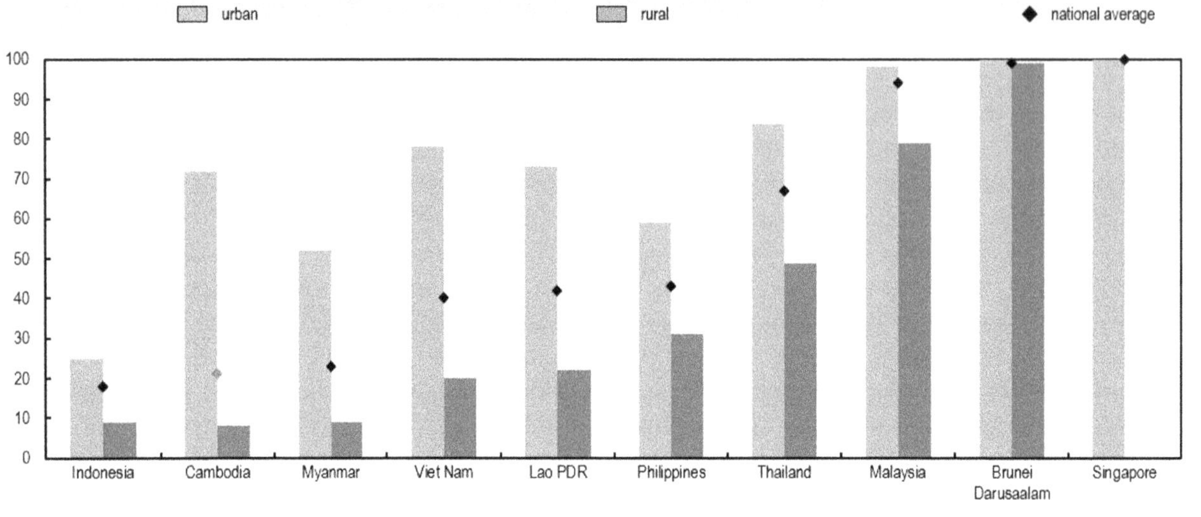

Source: Authors' elaboration based on (WHO/UNICEF, 2019[6]).

Solution

To facilitate access to finance of small-scale private water and electricity providers in rural areas of Cambodia, the AFD created the Access to Finance Project in 2014 (Figure A B.7). The Foreign Trade Bank of Cambodia (FTB) became the main commercial partner of the project by agreeing to take a concessional loan from AFD and risk-sharing guarantee (ARIZ) to expand its lending portfolio to the water and electricity sectors. The access to finance project aims at i) restructuring the financial sector to provide small-scale private operators with adequate loan products, and building their capacity to evaluate investment proposals; ii) reducing the risk associated with water service provision projects by improving business-brokering and engineering services in order to obtain large-enough loans; and iii) incentivising water operators to facilitate the connection of low-income households to reliable and safe water supply.

Figure A B.7. Access to Finance Project Cambodia financing structure

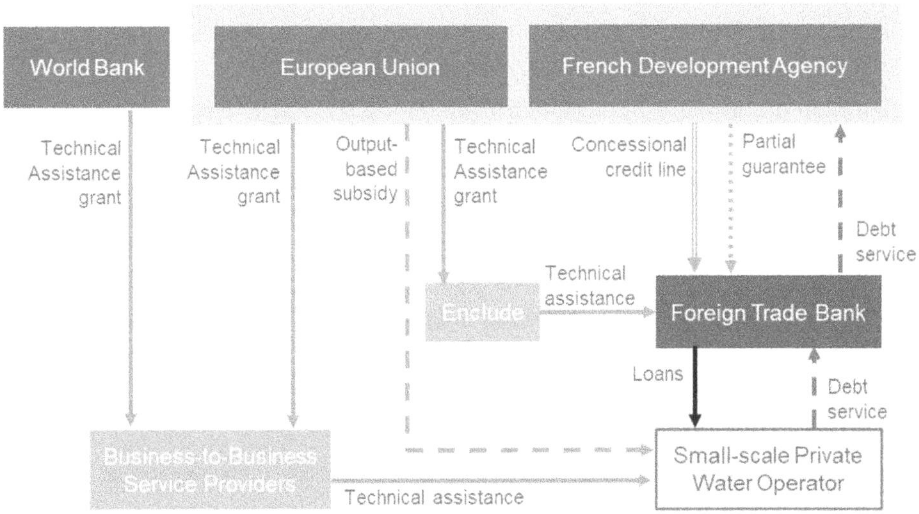

Source: Authors.

The AFD established a non-sovereign USD 15 million concessionary line of credit with FTB for loans in the water and electricity sectors, coupled with a risk-sharing guarantee (ARIZ). This allows the FTB to borrow from the AFD at lower costs compared with local financial options and reduces the collateral requirement in volume and in kind (formerly traditional mortgage-based lending were pooled with assets value and net present value) when lending to water and electricity operators.

The concessional nature of the credit line ensures that the financing is affordable to small and medium scale operators, with interest rates set at 6%-8% per annum on 10-year tenors inclusive of a 12-months grace period. To ensure that some of this fund is invested in the water sector, the FTB agreed to reserve one-third of the credit line for water operators. This agreement was later re-adjusted to two-thirds of the credit line (USD 10 million) because of high demand for water sector loans.

To securitise this line of credit, and lower the collateral requirements for small-scale borrowers, the AFD also set up a risk guarantee scheme through ARIZ, its mechanism to share loan portfolio risk between the AFD and FTB. The guarantee was set to USD 5 million in order to secure up to 50% of a USD 10 million loan portfolio.

Prior to the setting up of the credit line, the World Bank pre-financed the preparation of the business plan of the FTB providing grant funding to support water operators applying for FTB loans in developing business plans and engineering assistance. The World Bank also provided grant funding to improve the regulatory environment to improve transparency in the tariff and licensing practices of water operators.

The EU provided three kinds of grant, managed by the AFD:

i) A USD 0.7 million grant (EUR 0.6 million) to support TA (provided by Enclude) for FTB structuration, which aims at: i) improving the FTB's management capacities on commercial and technical skills required for the appraisal of infrastructures projects, particularly the methods for assessing the economic and financial rates of return; ii) improving of marketing, communications and information tools to supports the bank in developing an appropriate access-to-finance support service package dedicated to small-scale private water operators; iii) the development of the Environmental and Social Risk Management (ESRM) to be integrated in the bank's procedures.

ii) A USD 1.4 million grant (EUR 1.2 million) to finance technical assistance to small-scale private operators, aiming to foster an ecosystem of business-to-business services providers (engineering, business plan development, brokerage services) to drive small operators towards increased quality and professionalism. Several service providers were involved, led by GRET, including Innovative Services, Engineering and Advisory, Emerging Markets Consulting, and SeeSaw. These providers carried out support to the small-scale operators during the loan application process and ensured the quality of the business plan and overall project proposal.

iii) A USD 0.9 million grant (EUR 0.8 million) provided as a subsidy to encourage water operators to reduce and cap the cost of connecting poor households to a piped water supply system to USD 30 (the average connection fee stands at USD 64). Small-scale operators can choose to reduce this amount according to their marketing strategy, for which they can also receive assistance through the grant. The operators only receive the subsidy once the poor household is connected to a functioning metered connection. The grant also serves in assisting operators to improve their water quality management practices (i.e. conducting water quality analyses twice a week for 2 years) and in subsidising water quality equipment.

Moving forward, as the project nears completion, stakeholders are elaborating a strategy for the phasing out of the concessional finance. In order to transition from the blending of development finance with commercial financing towards less reliance on development finance, there is a need to cover critical technical assistance costs via the lending process itself. Before a loan is approved, it had to successfully get through the pre-financing process, organised along 3 stages: i) the water operators estimate their financial needs and request a loan to the FTB; ii) the FTB negotiates the loan amount based on the bankability of the project and risk profile of the operator, which are determined following a field visit and key indicators (business plan, balance sheet, financial statement). Once the agreement is reached, iii) water operators receive training on technical aspects, including to ensure the quality of the infrastructure resulting from the investment. The FTB may reject the loan request up to that stage. Technical assistance is thus key to reducing the risk of the project, however it is too costly for water operators to bear that cost. There is thus a need to diffuse that cost between the lender and the borrower without significantly raising the cost of the loan.

Impact

As of May 2019, most of the credit line had been consumed with a total of USD 10 million in water project loans disbursed across 30 projects, 27 of which were successfully completed.

The initiative led to:

- An increase in the performance and service quality of the projects financed, thanks to technical assistance funded by EU and to the pre-financing process followed by FTB to select sound projects. As a result, financed projects delivered better outcomes that were more aligned to the banks' expectations, which increased the bank's confidence in lending to the sector.
- Observed changes in lending practices as a result of the project, with the FTB adjusting its collateral requirement to not only include assets such as land or buildings, but also part of the appraised value of water infrastructure assets and part of the value of expected future revenue. This practice remains unique to the FTB in Cambodia.
- The creation of a new loan product in the market adapted to the needs of water service providers, with reduced interest (less than 8% per annum), a reduced collateral requirement from 200% to 100% of the loan thanks to the ARIZ risk sharing mechanism, and longer tenors (up to 10 years instead of 5 years).
- An increase in the number of households connected to a piped water system, including poor households. As of October 2018, 75 000 households benefited from water service improvements, of which an estimated 18 000 received new connections to a piped water system, including 8 000 poor households.

Although the project successfully achieved development objectives in terms of increasing access to piped water, the commercial financier had not fully addressed risk aversion to lending to water service providers. The project revealed that despite the liquidity risk cover and several layers of technical assistance offered to the bank and water operators, the attrition rate remained high (69%) between the number of loan requests (USD 32 million requested) and the rate of approval (USD 10 million disbursed). This resulted from the bank applying the same due diligence to loans of different amounts, and an average period of 6 months between the date of the loan request and that of the loan disbursement, conducive to a high rate of drop outs. Moving forward, there is a need to adapt the due diligence requirements based on the amount of the loan requested. These results also show the added value of an innovative business model, including a private business broker and technical assistance, which contributes to the creditworthiness of small-scale private operators. Finally, it shows how important confidence building is to the emergence of a mature investment environment in Cambodia.

Notes

[1] EAIF is a member of PIDG that mobilises public and private funds to lend to public and private infrastructure projects in Sub-Saharan Africa.

[2] The Cartagena Convention, adopted in 1983 and implemented in 1986, is a legal agreement between countries of the wider Caribbean region for the protection of the Caribbean Sea. The LBS protocol is one of three technical agreements supporting the convention, alongside the Protocols on Oil Spills and on Specially Protected Areas and Wildlife.

[3] Official exchange rate, 2015 period average, International Monetary Fund, International Financial Statistics.

[4] JICA merged with the development assistance section of the Japan Bank for International Cooperation (JBIC) on October 1, 2008.

[5] The source of the balloon payment will be a take-out loan from the Municipal Development Fund Office for Local Government Unit loans, and from DBP for Water District loans, executed under the same terms as the local bank's loan.

[6] The effective cost of borrowing for the ODA component was higher due to a 1% sovereign guarantee premium; a 3% foreign exchange cover; a 0.25% gross receipts tax; and a 3% mark up of DBP.

Annex C. Case Studies: Off-grid sanitation Water and Sanitation

Sanitation taxes for waste treatment plants and pay-for-success in desludging

Development finance

The Bill & Melinda Gates Foundation (BMGF) provides grant funding to the Centre for Environmental Planning and Technology (CEPT) University to develop research on the benefits and sustainable delivery modalities of integrated faecal sludge management and wastewater treatment. As a part of this, technical assistance provided by CEPT enabled municipal governments in Wai and Sinnar in the India State of Maharashtra to establish a sanitation tax as part of existing property taxes and introduce city-wide faecal sludge and septage management services. The approach uses a public-private partnership (PPP) to deliver scheduled emptying and establish faecal sludge treatment plants (FSTPs). The team is working with the State Government of Maharashtra to replicate and strengthen this model for application in cities state wide.

The local municipal government provided land to build the plants. In Wai, BMGF contributed grant funding towards the construction of a FSTP. In Sannar, the municipality used local resources to construct a plant. Revenues from the sanitation tax are used to pay for scheduled desludging contracts in both cities.

Commercial finance

In Wai and Sinnar, private sector operators for scheduled desludging were selected through a PPP tender. The company contracted to undertake scheduled desludging services used its own financing to provide the services city-wide in both urban areas.

In Wai, TIDE Technocrats, a domestic private company, was funded by BMGF to design, build, operate, transfer (DBOT) an innovative treatment facility as part of an effort to demonstrate the performance of new treatment approaches, ideally de-risking future procurement opportunities. In Sinnar, the private sector operator selected through a DBOT tender installed a more conventional facility.

The company contracted to undertake scheduled desludging services, once it had secured the government contract, independently pursued the necessary private financing to expand into these two new markets and establish city-wide services.

Challenge

As part of the 5-year Swachh Bharat Mission, the Government of India vowed to make its population Open Defecation Free (ODF) by October 2019. Maharashtra declared itself ODF in 2018. While this represented substantial progress, a lack of universal access to high quality sanitation services remains a major issue. In particular, systems for effective faecal sludge management need to be developed in small and medium-sized towns across the region.

Solution

CEPT's Centre for Water and Sanitation - in co-ordination with the state and the local government, as well as BMGF - have piloted integrated faecal sludge management and wastewater treatment systems in Wai and Sinnar. The pilot included the development of a ring-fenced sanitation tax, the establishment of PPP-based scheduled desludging services and grant funding to build a faecal sludge treatment plant (in Wai).

Technical assistance provided by CEPT funded by BMGF enabled both towns to establish a municipal sanitation tax as a part of its property tax system, which provides a predictable source of revenue. As a result, both municipal governments opened tender for a scheduled desludging service to all residential and non-residential properties. A private company won the desludging contract. The company is contracted for a three-year period to empty the septic tanks. The private company was not present in these town prior to the contract and invested its own capital to expand operations into the two new markets. The concession will be tendered after the three-year cycle. The scheduled emptying contracts in both cities use a performance-linked annuity model with a pay-for-results contract in place between the desludging company and local government. Payment is based on the number of septic tanks desludged, with an annual target specified in the contract. Figure A C.1 depicts the performance-linked annuity model for desludging services.

Figure A C.1. Performance linked annuity model for scheduled desludging services

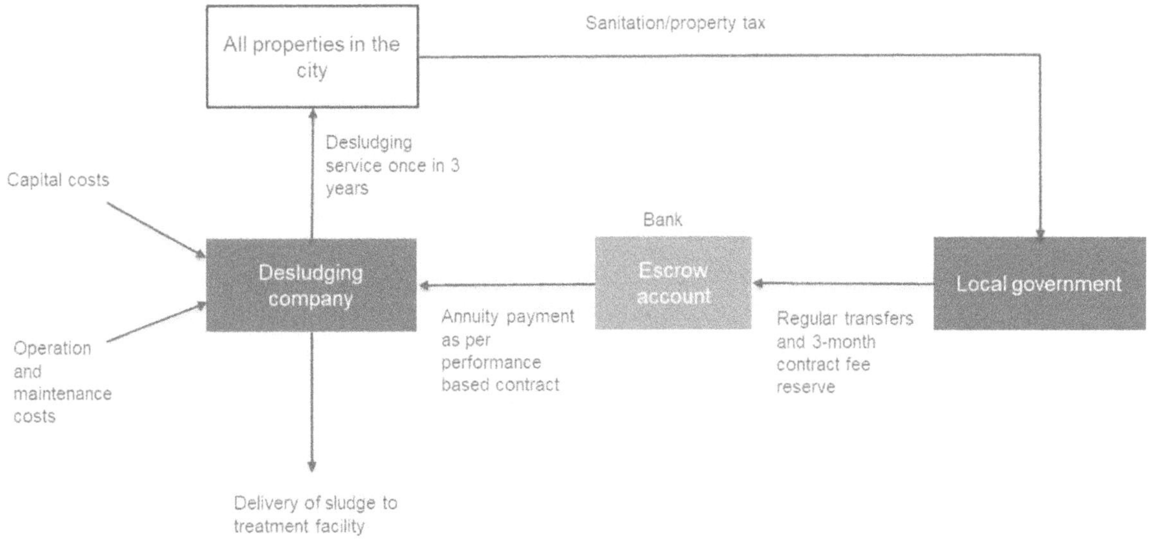

Source: Authors' elaboration based on (Bhavsar et al., 2019[8]).

In Wai, a FSTP was built by a local Indian company – TIDE Technocrats with funding from BMGF to demonstrate a new pyrolysis technology for the processing and reuse of waste. The land for the treatment plant was provided by the local government. The private company will operate the plant for two years with funding from BMGF. After this period, ownership of the plant will be transferred to Wai Council.

The town of Sinnar was able to fund the construction of waste treatment plant entirely from its own funds using grants received from the State Government. The private contractor for the FSTP in Sinnar was selected through a Design-Build-Operate (DBO) tender, with an operational period of three years.

Impact

The sanitation tax is structured to be progressive and payments are made incrementally. As a result, smaller properties pay less. The incremental payments and scheduled desludging has made the service more affordable to households (with some households paying approximately one-fifth of what they had previously paid). Wai was the first town in India to introduce a scheduled desludging system. Previously in both towns desludging was infrequent and usually done when septic tanks overflowed.

In Wai, over the past 12 months, 1 500 properties have received desludging services and over 4.8 million litres of septage has been delivered and treated at the FSTP. There is an acceptance rate of more than 93% by households for the scheduled service.

This project demonstrates an approach for small and medium towns in India to achieve universal sanitation. The success of the pilots in the two towns will inform state-level efforts in the development of regulatory frameworks and policies to overcome barriers to sanitation service provision. The success of pay-for-results scheduled desludging approach has led to discussions about how to scale up the provision of the service.

Currently, discussions with impact investors are ongoing about the potential of a development impact bond to demonstrate the possibility of attracting impact investments for such activities. The State Government plans to scale operations across more than 300 cities in Maharashtra. In the future, there is possibility to consider integrated contracts that combine scheduled emptying and FSTP construction and operations.

Funding waste water and faecal sludge treatment and reuse in Udaipur

Development finance

The Bill & Melinda Gates Foundation (BMGF) provided USD 1 million in grant funding to the Centre for Policy Research (CPR), for research and technical assistance in various geographies. This support influenced the decision of Udaipur Municipal Corporation to invest in faecal sludge management services and treatment plants instead of just sewerage systems. CPRs research played an important role in the development of the initial public private partnership for one faecal sludge treatment plant (FSTP) and a planned second plant.

Udaipur Municipal Corporation and Udaipur Improvement Trust rented the land to the private sector operator for the FSTP.

Commercial finance

Hindustan Zinc Ltd ([HZL], a Vedanta Group Company) provided 95% of financing for the original FSTP and committed to covering 100% of the operating costs for 5 years. In addition, they will finance 20% of the second planned faecal sludge treatment plant and 100% of the operating costs.

Challenge

Udaipur city is a municipal corporation in North Western region of India covering a total area of 64 km² and population of 451 735 as per the 2011 census. As of 2019, the city has high prevalence of septic tanks covering about 77.5% of households and low sewer network coverage, showing large deviation from the City Development Plan. Table A C.1 summarises the goals for sewerage services, which guide the construction of treatment facilities. As of 2014, only 20% of the city's population was covered by the network in place to dispose of, recycle and effectively treat waste.

Table A C.1. Sewerage service level goals

Components	Situation in 2014	Target for 2021	Target for 2031
Network coverage	20%	60%	100%
Treatment and disposal	20%	60%	100%
Recycle and reuse	20%	60%	100%
Operation & maintenance recovery	0%	60%	100%

Source: Undisclosed project documentation.

As per the City Development Plan, 22% of the city's total additional capital expenditure requirements would need to be allocated to investments in sewerage in order to meet the desired service level goal of universal sewerage coverage. In 2018, this amount was estimated to be 1 508 Rs Crore (approx. USD 250 million). This would equate to the highest share of the municipal capital expenditure needs, after water services. However, in spite of efforts to in source finance, thus far, sewers still serve only an estimated 20% of households in the city (approximately 91 322 inhabitants). Two new sewerage projects are under construction, to be operationalised in 2022. This would increase coverage up to 50% of the population.

Figure A C.2 further details gaps in the sanitation value chain in Udaipur. Notably, while access to toilets is above 90%, over 80% of waste produced in the city is not treated or reused.

Figure A C.2. Gaps in the sanitation value chain in Udaipur

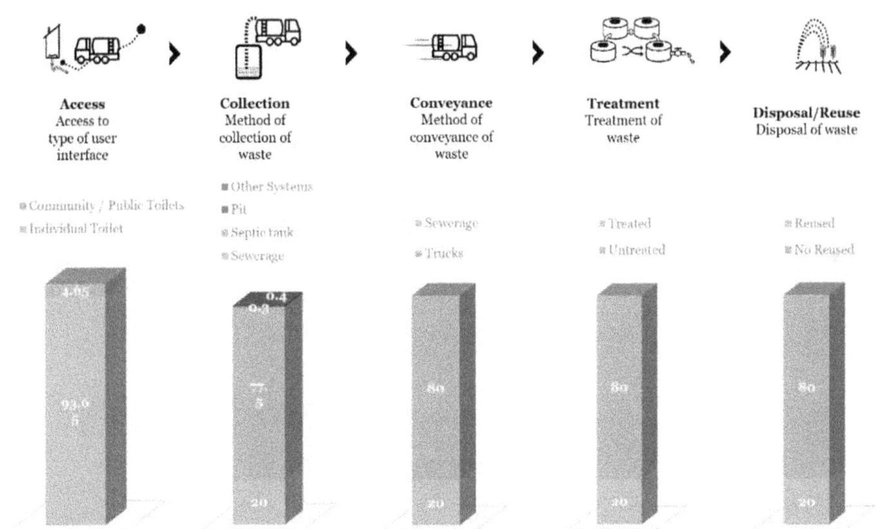

Source: Undisclosed project documentation.

Solution

In this context, the project "Partnering for MEWAR: Managing Environment through Waste Reuse" was conceptualised by the research centre CPR in partnership with local partners to introduce a specific system of improved faecal sludge and septage management in Udaipur. BMGF supported the CPR to help undertake research, a situational analysis, generate interest and participation of stakeholders and to support the project through technical advice. USD 300 000 was set aside for this research and stakeholder engagement. The project aims to build on an existing partnership between the public and private sectors to provide faecal sludge treatment and reuse.

Based on research, documentation and outreach under the project, the city is now implementing a comprehensive faecal sludge management improvement exercise with the support of stakeholders. In addition to financing and building the FSTP through a PPP arrangement, public investments are being made to ensure adequate/meaningful levels of collection and conveyance of sludge to the FSTP by investing in (a) procuring vacuum trucks, (b) the installation of GPS and licensing operators, (c) health and safety training to operators, (d) establishing FSM regulations in the city and (e) undertaking community awareness programs on the safe collection and treatment of faecal sludge.

Original public-private partnership

In 2014, a 20 million litre per day sludge treatment plant was commissioned with Udaipur Municipal Corporation and Urban Improvement Trust as parastatal agencies and Hindustan Zinc Limited (HZL) (a private mining and resources company operating in the region and headquartered in Udaipur) as concessionaire.

The plant was constructed on a design, build, own, operate and transfer (DBOOT) contract with a 25 year term period. The Urban Improvement Trust owns the land the plant was built on and gave HZL a lease to occupy it. The total project cost is INR 275 million with 95% of the cost borne by HZL for plant construction and 5% of the cost borne by Udaipur Improvement Trust for the land which was acquired for the project. The concessionaire operates the plant at its own cost and retains the right to reuse the treated wastewater for the duration of the project. To ensure sewerage supply to the plant from the city, Udaipur Municipal Corporation built a network including a 45 km trunk line with a cost of close to Rs 56 crores (approx. USD 9.5 million) connecting the sewered area of the city to the plant.

The contractual arrangement between the parties is illustrated in Figure A C.3 below.

Figure A C.3. Contractual and blended finance model of the Faecal Sludge Treatment Plant at Udaipur

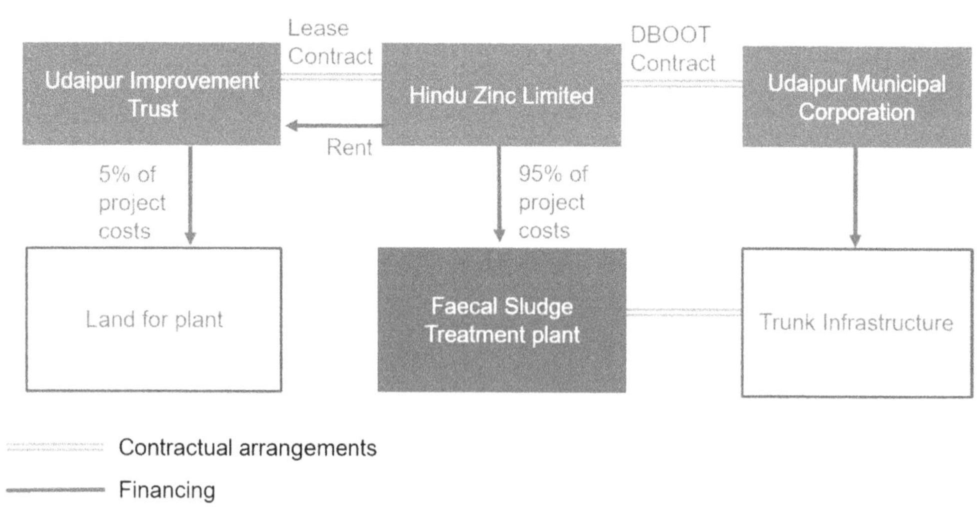

Source: Undisclosed project documentation.

Second faecal sludge treatment plant planned

Given the lag in the provision of sewerage services, a FSTP of 15 kilolitres per day (KLD) capacity is being developed to cover the requirements of the non-sewered parts of the city. This FSTP, based on thermo-chemical processes for treatment of faecal sludge, is under open bid process. Eighty percent of CAPEX is to be provided by the municipal government while 20% of CAPEX is provided by the concessionaire. The concessionaire, likely HZL, will be responsible for five years of OPEX for the faecal sludge treatment plant. The plant is expected to produce fly ash for soil conditioner and distilled water as by-products that can generate some revenue. The plant will also produce electricity, which will be used within the plant. The operator will have the rights to sell the treated by-products from the plant. A specific market study is currently ongoing, which will determine the extent of revenues that these by-products will generate (although they are not expected to cover operating costs). The project is structured as a design, build, own, operate and transfer (DBOT) project for a five-year initial term. The overall CAPEX will be around 0.85 million USD. This project will ensure that the current level of demand for faecal sludge treatment from across the city is met.

Impact

The MEWAR project is helping the local government and existing stakeholders in the sanitation sector in Udaipur to adopt alternative approaches for the safe treatment and reuse of sewerage to meet the service level targets for the city. It increased the understanding that almost 80% of households in the city do not have a planned, structured, formal access to safely managed sanitation. Furthermore, it educated stakeholders regarding the health risks citizens are exposed to due to the uncontrolled dumping of faecal sludge in open lands, drains and sometime water bodies.

This public funding of formalising, regulating, and monitoring safe collection, conveyance, and treatment of faecal sludge is strengthening and expanding private sector players' investments. In doing so, growth in service demand can be met. Also, facilitating investments in infrastructure—sewered and non-sewered—results in improved sanitation services.

BMGF's funding of the CPR's partnership with the city is supporting the city to learn how to engage in faecal sludge system management, establish meaningful incentives for continued operation of infrastructure, and most importantly, how to set and pursue meaningful expectations about improving sanitation service levels city-wide.

Water Credit and Water Equity: microfinance sanitation loans to expand access to sanitation in India

Development finance

Water.org provides grants and technical assistance and educational resources to microfinance institutions operating in the area in order for them to scale up sanitation loans

Commercial finance

Microfinance institutions disburse loans to households and, with the assistance and attention gained from involvement in the WaterCredit programme, attract investment from private investors. For example, KPMG in the case of the sanitation impact bond launched in 2018.

Challenge

As part of its 5-year sanitation campaign, the Government of India aims to make its population Open Defecation Free (ODF) by October 2019 and enacted a strategy that included a budget, state-level targets and awareness raising. A component of this budget is provided as an incentive to eligible households for toilet construction. These funds are typically offered after construction. As a result, cash reserves for up-front construction costs are needed.

Solution

Water.org's WaterCredit initiative facilitates household sanitation acquisition through partnership with local financial institutions. It provides technical assistance and project preparation funds to financial institutions to set up dedicated water and sanitation loan products for low-income borrowers. Under most circumstances, these institutions already lend to low-income people but are reluctant to lend specifically for water and/or sanitation due to perceptions of high repayment risk. The WaterCredit structure is designed to encourage these institutions to pilot water and sanitation lending, with the assumption that after confidence in the loan product's viability is built, they will mainstream it into their portfolios

The strategic use of technical assistance and/or a small grant from Water.org's philanthropic donors for project preparation – market assessment, loan product development, borrower education materials, etc. – aims to increase the outreach of sanitation services by mobilising household and commercial finance. In exchange for this assistance, the institution commits to loan targets within a given timeframe. During project preparation, tailored water and/or sanitation loan products are developed. The institution is responsible for sourcing its capital for on-lending. Approved clients receive the water and/or sanitation loan and repay it at market rates. The clients then use their loan to purchase and construct the water and/or sanitation asset.

Microfinance institutions report to Water.org on progress against the agreed-upon targets. Verification checks that the loan programme is active are done on an interval basis by third parties, and Water.org staff also conduct regular monitoring visits to assess progress and provide guidance.

As of 31 December 2018, Water.org has provided a total of USD 13 million in technical assistance and project preparation funds across its financial partners in India.

Figure A C.4. The WaterCredit Financing Structure

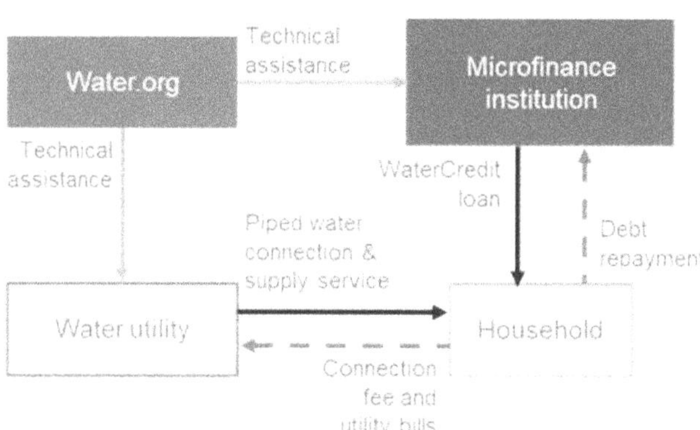

Source: Authors.

Impact

In turn, those partners have disbursed 2 089 887 locally-sourced loans totalling □USD 429 million □which have led to 9.4 million people accessing water (34%) and sanitation (66%). Products include toilets connected to septic tanks, bore wells and the installation of water connections. Repayment rates are 99%, even though (80%) of borrowers report incomes of less than USD 3.10 per day.

Cashpor Micro Credit, for example, started implementing WaterCredit in 2017. While they had been offering water and sanitation loans since 2012, the support from Water.org enabled them to improve collateral and training materials for staff. These efforts paid off: while Cashpor disbursed 80 000 water and sanitation loans in the five years before working with Water.org, within two years under the WaterCredit programme they disbursed 85 000 such loans and have expanded the water and sanitation lending across all five states where they have a presence.

At the same time, the programme has impacted the ability of some MFIs to attract additional sources of capital. Cashpor for example has been able to engage WaterEquity as an investor as well as attract capital via a Sanitation Impact Bond that was launched in 2018 by the Dutch partnership Finish Mondial (comprised of Actiam, Finish Society, KPMG, and WASTE). Finish Mondial's investment was strongly connected to Cashpor's activity with Water.org and WaterEquity.

Annex D. Case Studies: Multipurpose water infrastructure and landscape-based approaches

Municipal Water Conservation, Water Demand Management and Cost Recovery Programmes in South Africa

Development finance

The Development Bank of Southern Africa (DBSA) provided grant funding and technical assistance in the project preparation stage. The Infrastructure Investment Programme of South Africa (IIPSA) provided grant funding for the feasibility study. Grant funding from both DBSA and IIPSA will likely be involved in the financing of the project. DFIs are expected to part finance the project.

Commercial finance

Commercial investors are expected to partly finance the capital expenditure for the project.

Challenge

The City of Tshwane Metro ("the municipality") loses millions of rand annually due to water losses in the transmission and distribution network and poor cost recovery. Estimates of physical losses (leaks) in the municipality's network range between 25% and 40%. The impact of deteriorating water distribution and transmission infrastructure is not limited to physical losses only. In an environment of limited maintenance, water meters are typically the type of device where maintenance falls short or is neglected completely. As a result, the proportion of non-functional water meters is growing rapidly. This has a direct impact on billing and cost recovery. Inadequate management systems, lack of capacity, poor credit control, consumer resistance to pay more for services due to poor service levels as well as corrupted databases are all contributing factors to poor cost recovery. A turnaround of the status quo is required. However, significant capital is required to implement a holistic municipal Water Conservation and Water Demand Management Programme (WCWDM). Thus, funding for such a programme will often not fit within standard balance sheet financing instruments given debt sustainability issues and requires an alternative financing approach.

Solution

The envisaged financing approach for the programme is a hybrid between conventional balance sheet finance and project finance. The intention is to strengthen the financial position of the municipality over the programme duration. This will be achieved by generating alternative future cash flows stemming from the interventions that are implemented on a sub-project level. Funding for future sub-projects will be progressively advanced to the municipality in tranches by the participating financiers against strict criteria for the achievement and maintenance of key performance indicators of the sub-projects already implemented. As the programme is rolled out, less debt will be required to finance the new sub-projects as the municipality will be able to fund a larger portion through own funds generated from the savings and improved revenues stemming from already implemented sub-projects.

Figure A D.1. Envisaged funding structure

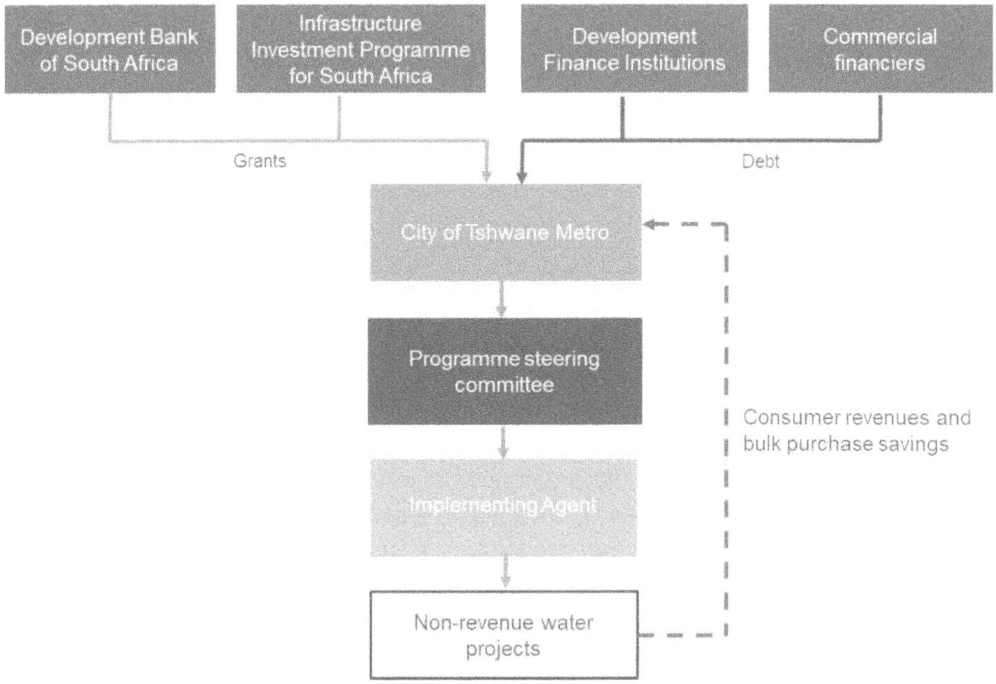

Source: Undisclosed project documentation.

The programme under development consists of a number of sub-projects that will cover a distinct supply area (also termed a district metering area [DMA]). Each DMA will be able to be managed and monitored on a continuous basis, including the monthly rolling annual water balance estimates, ongoing active leak detection, as well as tracking of financial performance. To implement the programme, each of sub-projects will be rolled out sequentially. The performance of sub-projects that already implemented can then be monitored and verified on a continuous basis. The overarching aim is an integrated approach across the various municipal functions and divisions to ensure financial benefits with regard to the key performance and strategic measures. These include the reduction of the recoverable real losses, reduction in over-consumption and improved cost recovery. The programme will consists of two phases (pre- and post-financial close) as outlined in Figure A D.2.

Figure A D.2. Programme outline

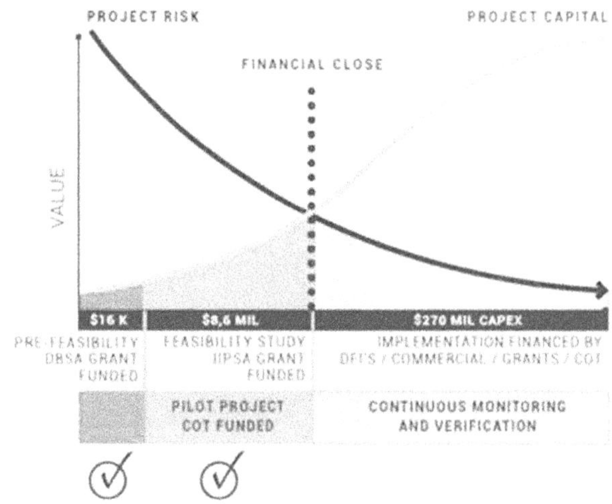

Source: Undisclosed project documentation.

Phase 1 of the programme focusses on the preparation stage up to financial close in order to identify, assess and mitigate all of the relevant risks. The bankable feasibility study is currently underway and will contain detailed recommendations on the technical, institutional, legal, and financial risks. The recommendations in the feasibility study will impact the final definition and implementation of the programme, and needs to be approved by the municipal council. This will form the basis of the future credit evaluation and approval process for the financing and implementation of the identified sub-projects in the programme.

Impact

One of the main conclusions from the holistic approach to WCWDM programme methodology is that it allows for the deferment of significant investment in bulk supply infrastructure by expediting the programme implementation period. The impact assessment is yet to be concluded but it is anticipated that the key benefits for the municipality will include reduced water losses in the distribution system, reduction in over consumption and improved billing and cost recovery rates.

Jordan Compact - Blended finance and the expansion of the As-Samra Wastewater Treatment Plant

Development finance

The Millennium Challenge Cooperation (MCC) provided technical assistance and viability gap funding for the expansion of As-Samra Wastewater Treatment Plant.

The Government of Jordan under the compact agreed to partly finance the expansion of the wastewater treatment plant and related projects.

Commercial finance

Suez contributed equity financing to the special purpose vehicle for the expansion of the wastewater treatment plant and raised USD 110 million in debt financing from a syndicated loan arranged by Arab Bank.

Challenge

Jordan is one of the driest countries in the world and is facing severe water shortages. Jordan is a relatively resource poor country with no oil or natural gas, and only around 3% arable land. With limited access to surface water, Jordan ranks among the world's most water scarce countries. Population growth projections suggest that on a per capita basis, available fresh water supplies are expected to decline significantly over the next 15 years, increasing the risk of higher water costs impacting households and industrial productivity.

Solution

MCC (a US aid agency) and Jordan signed a USD 275.1 million five-year compact in 2010, addressing the growing water needs of the Zarqa Governorate. Zarqa is the third largest Governorate of the Country and experiencing rapid growth in population as well as industrial and commercial activity. The objective of the MCC investment in Jordan was to maximise economic growth by making more fresh water available for municipal and industrial use. This was accomplished through three projects to promote water substitution and water saving:

1. The Water Network Expansion Project (water savings) with the objective of reducing water losses from the secondary and tertiary network and making more water available in the system. High-quality treated effluent from As-Samra is now conveyed to the Jordan Valley for use in agricultural production.
2. The Wastewater Network Expansion Project (water substitution), which was designed to collect more household wastewater through expanding the network to previously unserviced areas.
3. Expansion of the As-Samra Wastewater Treatment Plant (water substitution)[1] to provide the treatment capacity for the additional wastewater collected with the Wastewater Network Expansion Project. High-quality treated effluent from As-Samra is conveyed to the Jordan Valley for use in agricultural production. Freshwater used in Jordan Valley is conveyed to Amman and Zarqa for municipal and industrial use.

The As-Samra Wastewater Treatment Plant in Jordan was constructed in 2008 with support from USAID. However, the wastewater treatment plant was overburdened and required capacity expansion. The MCC committed to assist the Ministry of Water and Irrigation (MWI) in Jordan by conducting advisory services and at the same time viability gap funding of a USD 93 million in the form of a grant. The current private operator Suez, a French multinational, submitted a proposal that mobilised funding from the Arab Bank contingent on the grant funding from MCC. The viability gap funding for the brownfield project and a USD 20 million grant for the Government enabled Suez to raise USD 110 million in private financing arranged by the Arab Bank through a loan syndication process involving Jordanian local banks and other financial institutions. The syndicated loan is Jordanian dinar-denominated and has a tenor for 13 years with the option to extend to 20. This was the longest maturity that had been obtained for a Jordanian dinar-denominated loan in 2012. While the interest rate during the three-year construction period for the treatment plant expansion was fixed, following the commissioning of the plant, the loan evolved to a floating rate linked to the average prime lending rate of four local banks.

The expansion was conducted through a build-operate-transfer (BOT) contract, a form of public-private partnership (PPP). The BOT contract was signed between MWI and Samra Wastewater Treatment Plant Company Limited (SPC); consortium members include Suez, Morganti and Infilco Degrémont. The total project cost for the expansion of the treatment plant was USD 223 million, with the private sector covering over 50% of the cost. SPC will operate and maintain the plant for 25 years. The presence of a private partner Suez, with experience successfully operating the treatment plant, from the outset provided security and reduced the perception of risk and actual risks for the additional investors. At the end of the concession period, in 2037, the agreement requires that the facility be transferred back to the Government of Jordan for free and in good working order. The financing structure is illustrated in Figure A D.3.

Figure A D.3. Viability financing for the As-Samra Wastewater Treatment Plant expansion: Financial structure

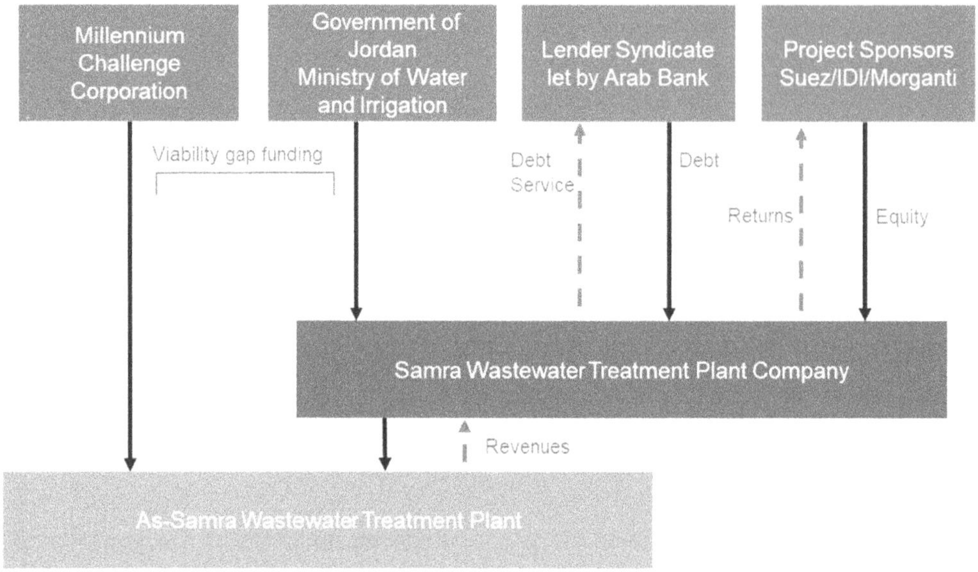

Source: (World Bank, 2016[9])

The Water Network Project was composed of two parts; infrastructure investment in transmission and distribution pipes and improvements in the quality of plumbing in the homes of 3 958 poor families as well as schools. The infrastructure investment activity rehabilitated 864.7 kilometres of water pipes, built a new pump station, and installed 41 650 household water meters. It established more efficient district metering areas, enabling better operation and management of the water utility. The activity is also expected to contribute to a decline in commercial and physical water losses from 61.6% to 50.7% across the Zarqa Governorate. The reduction of physical losses will improve the cost recovery of the Zarqa water utility and a result the utility expects to achieve full cost recovery by 2019.

The Waste Water Network Project extended service to households that were not connected to the sewer network by constructing over 300 kilometres of new sewers in the neighbourhoods of East Zarqa and West Zarqa. The extension raised wastewater service coverage rates from 72% to approximately 84% of the estimated Jordanian population. In addition, USD 18.9 million of unused budget from the Water Network Project was used to add 65 kilometres of sewage collection pipes to the Princess Haya neighbourhood of the Zarqa and to purchase high pressure jet cleaning vehicles for the water utility to enhance system maintenance.

Impact

The expansion allowed the Government to treat 70% of the country's wastewater and provides 109 million cubic meters of treated water per year for irrigation in the Jordan Valley. In addition, the As-Samra plant has improved the long-term sludge management and disposal practices further helping to preserve Jordan's water resources.

At the end of the Compact between the Government and MCC, approximately 375 000 households (2 023 000 individuals) had benefitted 2010-15 from additional supplies of freshwater released as larger volumes wastewater were used for agricultural production in the Jordan Valley. Approximately 8 500 households in the Jordan Valley or 46 000 individuals now receive a consistent supply of high-quality treated wastewater that can be used for irrigation. The As-Samra plant also provides bio-solids for potential reuse in fertilizer and fuel, and produces 80% of its own energy needs, from biogas and hydropower. The plant is as a result one of the most energy efficient treatment plants in the Middle East. In addition, the involvement and grant funding from MCC helped reduced the cost of capital, which in turn allowed for lower tariff to consumers.

However, whilst the expansion and related compact projects have been successful, the new plant is already nearing full capacity. The intention to expand the plant again with funding from the EU and EBRD was announced in December 2018. A deal is expected to be finalised with the Ministry of Water and Irrigation.

Multipurpose Hydropower Project in Lao People's Democratic Republic (PDR)

Development finance

Lao People's Democratic Republic (PDR), World Bank, Asian Development Bank (ADB), Nordic Investment Bank, French Development Agency (AFD), Proparco, European Investment Bank (EIB)

Commercial finance

The Nam Theun 2 Power Company (25% Lao PDR, 40% Électricité de France [EDF] , 35% Electricity Generating Public Company Limited), EDF, Export-Import Bank of Thailand, Export Credit Agencies (COFACE EKN, GIEK) and seven Thai commercial banks (Bangkok Bank, Bank of Ayudhya, Kasikornbank, Krung Thai Bank, Siam City Bank, Siam Commercial Bank and Thai Military Bank).

Challenge

Lao People's Democratic Republic is a landlocked country that was one of the poorest countries in the East Asia region in 2003 with human development indicators among the lowest in the region (World Bank, 2018[10]). With extensive water resources, the development of hydropower was key pillar of government plans for economic growth and the achievement of poverty reduction targets. However, constraints such as limited government financing capacity, lack of experience of developing large scale hydropower projects for export and limited ability to attract private sector investment hindered the development of hydropower infrastructure.

Solution

The idea for a large scale hydropower project, Nam Theun 2 (NT2), was three decades in making, with the World Bank first recommending that the Government of Lao undertake a feasibility study to assess the potential for a power station in 1988. The feasibility study was conducted in 1991 (MacGeorge, 2009[11]). In 1994, EDF and the Italian-Thai Development Company of Thailand started the project. Thus, NT2 moved from a conceptual to a development phase. The design and preparation of a complete set of economic, environmental and social safeguards took more than ten years.

The Government of Lao prepared a National Growth and Poverty Eradication Strategy in 2003, which focused on the need to create sustained economic growth to achieve poverty reduction. The large scale hydropower project NT2 was a key part of the strategy. The purpose of NT2 was to generate electricity from hydropower for export to the Electricity Generating Authority of Thailand (EGAT). In addition, there was a social and environmental management programme, which included wildlife management and watershed protection (4 000 km2 of forested watershed, which ensures a continuous supply of water to the reservoir). Project financing was gradually put in place and full construction activities commenced in June 2005.

The NT2 hydropower project aimed to produce 1 070 MW, providing 995 MW of power for export, and 75 MW for domestic consumption. A 25 year power purchase agreement (PPA) was signed between the Nam Theun Power Company, Electricity Generating Authority of Thailand (EGAT) and Électricité du Lao – the state-owned power company of Lao PDR. The agreement conditions included the sale of 5 636 GWh/year to EGAT at a predefined tariff, which is paid half in US dollars and half in local currency in order to mitigate currency risks and avoid local currency devaluation.

The USD 1 300 million project is the world's largest private sector hydroelectric project financing. A special purpose company, the Nam Theun 2 Power Company (NTPC) was created as a public-private partnership (PPP), which is partly controlled by the government which has a 25% stake. The government of Lao PDR and NTPC signed a concession agreement in 2002 contracting NTPC to finance, develop, construct, own, and operate the hydroelectric plant and facilities for 25 years. The financial closure of the project and environmental and social programme occurred in December 2017. After the 25-year period, the plant will be transferred back to the government free of charge (it is a Build, Own, Operate, Transfer [BOOT] project).

Due to the large scale of the project, the financing plan was complex, with 27 institutions involved (see Figure A D.4.) including MDBs, DFIs, Export Credit Agencies (ECAs) and Thai banks. A range of instruments were used to mobilise private finance including guarantees, grants and debt. Around 85% (over USD 1 000 million) of the total financing for capital costs of the scheme was mobilised by the private sector. USD 350 million raised through ECA's with partial guarantees from IDA and MIGA. Thai commercial banks provided USD 500 million in local currency debt financing towards the project. In terms of equity financing, the Government of Lao invested USD 93 million, which came from a mix of concessionary grants and loans from the World Bank's IDA fund, EIB, ADB and AFD. EDF contributed USD 131 million in equity financing.

In addition, USD 78.6 million was provided by NTPC to cover the costs of the social and environmental management programme, including resettlements of affected populations, social services, environmental protection, wildlife management and watershed protection.

Figure A D.4. Stylised financing scheme – Nam Theun 2

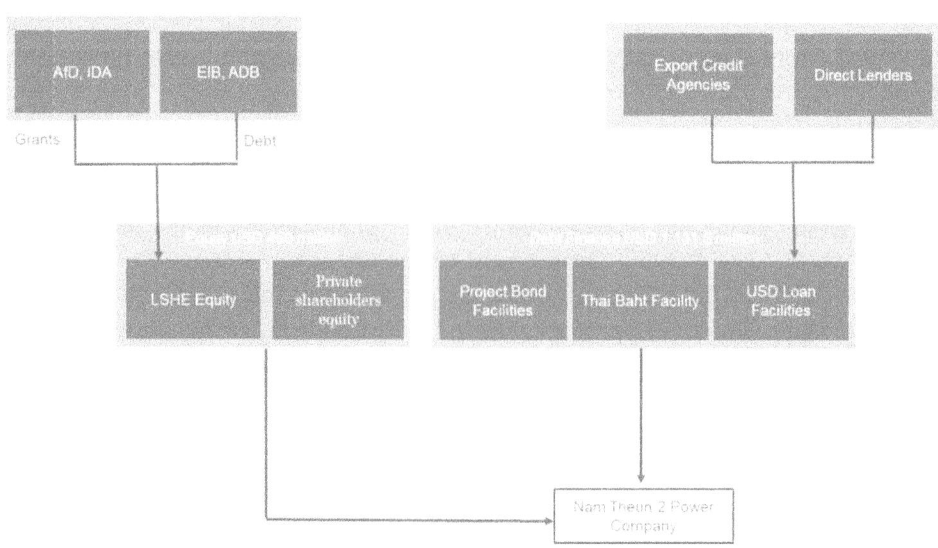

Source: Authors based on (Naughton, DeSantis and Martoussevitch, 2017[12]).

The project was repeatedly delayed and faced many setbacks (World Bank, 2010[13]). These included equity owners selling stakes, and the transfer of responsibility of the BOT contract from Transfield Holdings to EDF. In addition, the Asian financial crisis in 1997 led to delays in project development and re-negotiation of the PPA between the government and EGAT; the project was originally scheduled to be built by 2000 but delays meant that the government could not fulfil the contract with EGAT. In terms of private financing, two equity investors representing 20% of equity financing sold their holdings mid-way through the process.

Designs for the project went through several phases with the original hydropower plants on a smaller scale. The cost of the project was also revised several times. First, the cost was revised upward from the original estimation of USD 900 million to USD 1.1 billion. Later, it was revised upwards again to USD 2 billion. However, the onset of the 1997 Asian financial crisis and concerns from investors led NPTC to revise the costs down to USD 1.3 billion.

Impact

The NT2 hydropower plant began commercial operations in 2010. The power generated is exported to Thailand and used domestically. Over USD 170 million in revenue was received by the Lao treasury in income from the project between 2010 and 2017. In line with legal agreements, all revenue is allocated to projects and programmes contributing to poverty reduction or environmental management. The education and health sectors received the largest shares of revenue, with 39% and 14% of total revenue disbursed (see Table A D.1).

Table A D.1. Disbursement of NT2 Government Revenues

Sector	Million USD	Percentage
Education	65.81	35.3
Health	62.14	33.3
Public Works and Transport	15.67	8.4
Energy, Mining and Agriculture	24.32	13.1
Natural Resources and Environment	1.31	0.7
Poverty Reduction Fund	9.91	5.3
Projects Implemented by Provinces	7.05	3.9
Total	186.22	100

Source: State Audit Organization (SAO) Audit Reports 2009/10 - 2015/16, MoF Data FY15/16 and FY17 & World Bank 2018, Implementation Completion and Results Report – Nam Theun 2. (World Bank, 2018[10])

In addition, significant efforts were made to mitigate the negative externalities of the project. Environmental and social management plans for the project include the establishment of long term watershed protection and management systems for the Nakai Nam Theun National Protected Area and associated corridors; compensatory forestry to offset the loss of primary forest in the reservoir; livelihood development initiatives for people to be resettled, with clearly-specified poverty reduction objectives; and reservoir fisheries managed by local people, with extensive independent monitoring, including penalties for non-compliance. Resettlement villages and farms have been established and compensation for livelihood losses resulting from the river diversion has been carried out. For example, all of the 6 300 people displaced by the project were resettled and 100% of them met the income target of reaching at least the rural poverty level.

Water funds: A financial, technical and institutional mechanism that promotes public and private sector participation for watershed conservation.

Development finance

Inter-American Development Bank (IADB), The Nature Conservancy (TNC), FEMSA Foundation, the Global Environment Facility (GEF) provide grant funding and technical assistance to set up and scale Water Funds as well as technical assistance for project development.

Commercial finance

The source of funding from commercial actors and level of funding is different for each water fund. Funding from commercial actors, such as corporates, is usually sourced from companies operating within the spatial area with a stake in improved water resource management. For instance, Heineken operates a brewery in Monterrey and plays a large role in funding the Monterrey Metropolitan Water Fund.

Challenge

Despite numerous efforts to improve watershed management, few programs provide the legal and financial mechanisms to allocate funding for water source conservation and climate adaptation. On the one hand, protected areas, which in many cases were originally created to shelter water sources, often lack the financial support needed for conservation activities in upstream farmlands. In Colombia, for example, 50% of the population receives water from public protected areas, but market and institutional failures prevent these areas from getting the necessary financial resources to be soundly managed. On the other hand, upstream private and communal lands that provide hydrologic, environmental and climate adaptation services are typically not compensated by downstream users. Current incentives often lead to upstream farmers continue to employ land practices that negatively affect water quantity and quality. In most cases, it would be more cost-effective to compensate farmers to improve their land practices, set aside private areas for conservation or improve the management of public protected areas than bear the costs of poorly managed water resources. Access to predicable and sufficient funding is critical to implement improved watershed management. Thus, there is a need to establish financial and institutional mechanisms to provide downstream users the incentive and opportunity to proactively engage in conservation and climate adaptation practices in upstream catchment areas. Such interventions help to balance upstream and downstream interests within the watershed for water and land use.

Solution

Water Funds provide a financial, technical and institutional mechanism that promotes public and private sector participation for watershed conservation. This mechanism offers opportunities to promote the sustainable management of watersheds and improved water security for downstream users, whether they are city dwellers, corporates or agricultural users. The water funds model, first set up by TNC and the Municipality of Quito, brings together different types of public and private actors in a pooling mechanisms that provide long-term, sustainable finance to contribute to water security through nature-based solutions.

Since that initial effort, IADB, in partnership with TNC, the FEMSA Foundation, and GEF launched the Latin American Water Funds Partnership in 2011. The partnership creates and strengthens Water Funds across the Latin American region to improve watershed management. The partnership started with USD 21 million (USD 5 million from an IADB - GEF grant, USD 6 million grant from the FEMSA Foundation, and USD 10 million from other supporters through TNC). Since 2011 the partnership has created and strengthened 24 Water Funds across the region.

In June 2016, IADB, GEF, TNC and the FEMSA Foundation launched the second phase of the Water Funds Partnership in Bogota for the 2016-20 period. Thus far, more than USD 150 million from 215 public and private organisations have been provided to nature-based solutions via the Water Funds.

Water Funds provide funding for a range of activities related to watershed management. These include: (i) feasibility studies; (ii) conservation projects; (iii) monitoring and evaluation; (iv) endowment; (v) governance, technical assistance, and communication products. The conservation projects can be grouped in three categories: (i) payment for environmental services, including watershed management and biodiversity conservation; (ii) water resource management such as sustainable land use; and (iii) conservation projects for further protection of the natural habitat where these services originate. These categories include the creation of protected areas, reforestation, helping landowners switch to conservation-friendly practices, and supporting community-driven conservation initiatives.

While contributions to the water funds do not generate financial returns to capital providers, the benefits of more effective watershed management can attract capital contributions from large water users such as water supply companies, hydropower plants, irrigation districts, agricultural associations and other private sector actors, such as breweries and soft drink companies. Large water supply companies for instance benefit as improvements in water quality result in reduced treatment costs. This can lead to significant savings in terms of avoided costs in large urban centres that may exceed conservation investments. Similarly, investments in nature-based solutions to manage watersheds can reduce the recurring costs for hydropower plants by reducing sediment accumulation and silting of dams. The only TNC supported water fund that has mobilised repayable financing so far is in the US, San Antonio, Texas.

Figure A D.5. The Water Fund Endowment Model

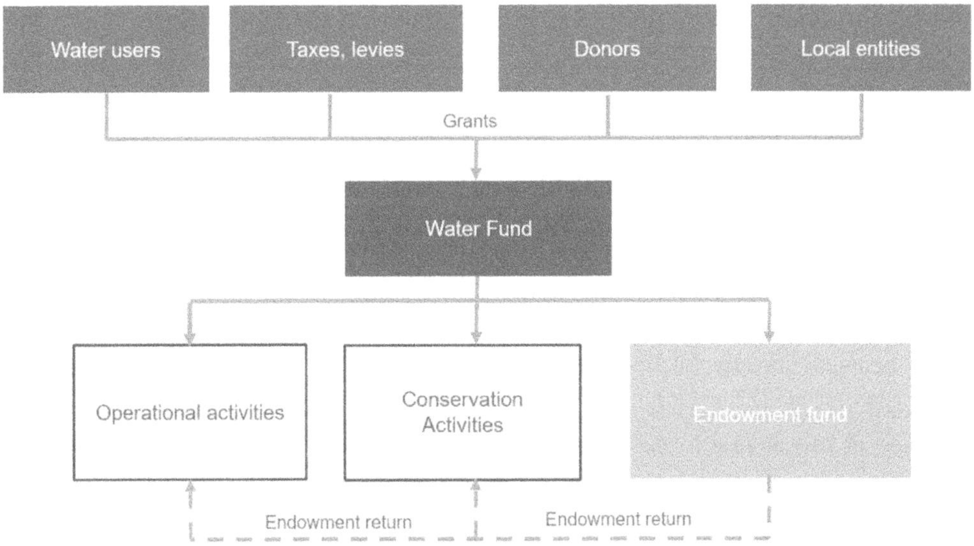

Source: (TNC, 2011[14]).

Many of the existing water funds in Latin America have developed an “endowment fund” approach (see Figure A D.5), whereby philanthropy funding is used to capitalise a fund and proceeds from investing those funds are used for annual investments in nature-based conservation. A notable example is the Fondo Para La Protección Del Agua (FONAG) in Ecuador.

Water funds can have a variety of funding sources. For example, the Monterrey Metropolitan Water Fund (FAMM) in Mexico is predominantly funded by private capital, with over 75% of the funds provided by the private sector, with the remainder of funding provided by bilateral and multilateral development agencies. Heineken operates a brewery within the region and provides funding for FAMM. The fund was set up in

2013 to increase the water security for the city of Monterrey located on the banks of the Santa Catarina River. Over 60% of the water used in the metropolitan areas derives from Cumbres de Monterrey National Park, located within the San Juan River Basin. In the basin, soil erosion and the loss of vegetation cover have negatively impacted run off control. In addition, changes in land use and forest have also contributed to the degradation of the water supply to Monterrey metropolitan area. The region is also prone to hurricanes which can have further devastating effects on the city. FAMM funds reforestation, restoration and soil management to improve water infiltration in the San Juan River Basin and to reduce the potential impact of natural disasters. FAMM has more than 40 partners including the federal government, local government, businesses and NGOs. As of 2016, USD 8 million had been pledged by the private sector to FAMM.

Impact

After five years spreading the water fund concept, the partnership found that five elements (inclusion, scalability, fundability, adaptability, and stack ability) enable multi-stakeholder collaboration in a way that allows for activities to go beyond simply conservation, but to pursue watershed sustainability over the long-term.

In total, the Latin American Water Funds Partnership implemented by the IADB has led to the creation of 24 Water Funds and the implementation of watershed conservation projects that have potentially benefitted 89 million people as of June 2018. In addition, 525 684.5 hectares of natural habitat has been conserved or positively impacted by water fund operations (The Latin American Water Funds Partnership, 2018[15]). The aim is for the programme to continue to expand and generate collective action towards water security.

Infrastructure Services and Renewables Projects - Transforming Bugala Island's Infrastructure

Development finance

Four organisations affiliated with the Private Infrastructure Development Group (PIDG) helped to finance the project at different stages of its development:

- The Emerging Africa Infrastructure Fund[2] (EAIF) provided USD 9.4 Million in debt financing.
- InfraCo Africa provided USD 11.8 million of equity funding.
- PIDG's Technical Assistance Facility (TAF) provided a USD 6.04 million grant to cover upfront capital costs incl. USD 5 million of output based aid to fund ferry and water connections.
- GuarantCo in co-operation with USAID provided a guarantee that was critical in attracting commercial finance from NedBank.

In addition, the Uganda Development Committee contributed USD 9.9 million in equity funding and the Industrial Development Corporation of South Africa, USD 11.4 million.

Commercial finance

USD 5.2 million debt financing from Nedbank was guaranteed jointly by GuarantCo and USAID (GuarantCo, 2011[16]).

Challenge

Bugala Island is the largest of 84 islands that make up the Ssese archipelago in Lake Victoria, covering 275 square km. Bugala Island was previously one of Uganda's poorest districts and had a prevalent shortage of potable water. The majority of the population used lake water, which is not safe for bathing and consumption (Valahu, 2015[17]). In addition, the existing pipe network in Kalangala town was in poor condition and in need of replacement.

Solution

In 2005 InfraCo Africa established the Kalangala Infrastructure Investment Services (KIS) to address these issues. KIS operates as a multi-donor public-private partnership with the KIS responsible for the investment and maintenance of the infrastructure for 15 years. The government signed a memorandum of understanding with InfraCo in 2006. In January 2009, following the approval of Cabinet of the InfraCo project development plan, KIS and the Government of Uganda entered into an Implementation Agreement.

The KIS investment in water infrastructure was part of a broader multi-sector initiative, aiming to improve access to water, safer transportation, and more reliable, renewable (solar powered) electricity. The project had four infrastructure components; including the development of two passenger ferries and the development of a 1.6 MW Solar-Thermal hybrid power generating station, water infrastructure investment and road upgrade (Valahu, 2015[17]). The total investment for the four projects was USD 54 million in addition to USD 6.3 million for project development costs.

In respect to water infrastructure, the project involved:

- Rehabilitation of the existing transmission and distribution piped water system in Kalangala Town. Expansion of the network will entail installing pipes and standpipes to areas currently not served by the piped water network.
- Creation of a water treatment plant in Mweena Village designed to treat 418 cubic metres a day with a rated output of 376 cubic metres a day (the difference being for plant use).
- KIS operates the water treatment plant providing the water at a tariff rate agreed between KIS and the Government.

The special purpose vehicles KIS and Kalangala Renewables were created and the project was financed through a PPP.

KIS was financed with a commercial loan of USD 3.3m from Nedbank as well as a combination of debt and equity from various DFIs, including EAIF and a joint debt guarantee from USAID/GuarantCo. TAF provided an output based aid (OBA) grant of USD 5 million, used initially to fund the ferry construction and then reallocated to subsidise power and water connections as well as the ferry service to poor households on Bugala Island. OBA grant of USD 1.7 million for KIS was directly targeted at enabling affordability for the local, poorer community. InfraCo Africa maintains a 54% equity stake in the project.

Kalangala Renewables funded its investment with an OBA grant from TAF of USD 3.3 million and a USD 1.8 million commercial loan from Nedbank, alongside DFI loans and equity funding totalling USD 13.8 million, including USD 2.4 million from EAIF. InfraCo Africa will maintain a 54% equity stake in the project. Both projects reached financial close in December 2012.

Collective financing breakdown for both projects:

- USD 6.3 million in development costs; USD 6.04 million in grants, of which USD 5 million is OBA;
- USD 5.2 million debt financing from Nedbank which benefitted from a joint GuarantCo and USAID guarantee;
- USD 42.5 million by development finance institutions divided in: USD 33.1m in the form of equity from 1) Uganda Development Committee (USD 9.9 million); 2) Industrial Development Corporation of South Africa (USD 11.4 million); and 3) PIDG though InfraCo Africa (USD 11.8 million); USD 9.4 million debt financing from EAIF.

Figure A D.6 Kalangala financing model

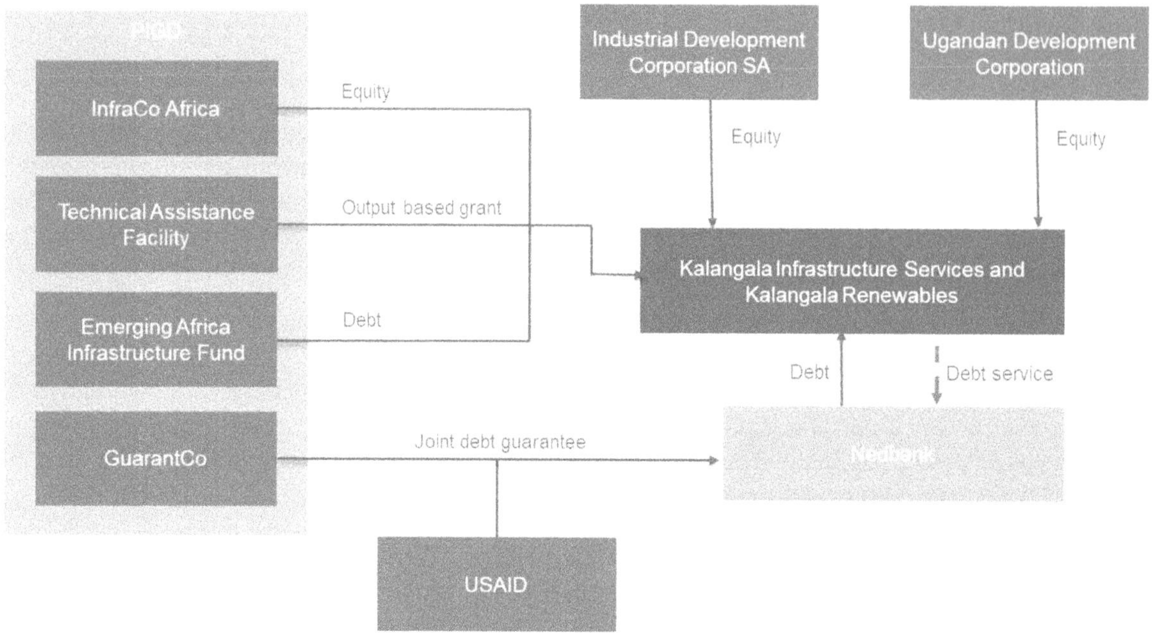

Source: Authors.

Impact

KIS constructed the Mwena water treatment plant, which has a capacity of producing over 400 000 litres of water per day and the reservoir tanks/storage facilities of 200 000 litres. The improvement has enabled KIS to supply water to Bugala Island 24 hours a day. As a result of safe water supply services, the population on Bugala Island has experienced a reduction in medical expenses due to reduction water in borne diseases and improved sanitation. Those villages now supplied with clean, safe water have seen an 80% drop in waterborne disease.

In addition, the multi-sector nature of the project has enabled it to have a much larger impact on living standards than each element could have achieved in isolation. The project will provide much needed access to infrastructure for the Bugala inhabitants, which will have further effects on economic development - including provision of tourism and on the fishing which is traditionally one of the main industries - and quality of life.

The project took InfraCo Africa seven years to develop and reach financial close. During this time it has contributed to several improvements in the regulatory environment including the creation of the first private sector water authority in Uganda.

Improving the financial viability of the Songwe River Basin Development Programme through the use of blended finance

Development finance

The Government of Tanzania and the Government of Malawi are jointly engaged in development plan for the Songwe River Basin. Both governments are expected to contribute equity financing to the programme.

In collaboration with the Climate Resilient Infrastructure Development Facility, the Africa-EU Water Partnership Programme being implemented by the Stockholm International Water Institute (SIWI) is supporting the Songwe River Basin Commission to mobilise blended financing for the Songwe River Basin Development Programme.

The Africa-EU Water Partnership Project is a joint undertaking by the European Union, the African Ministers Council on Water and the Government of Sweden through Sida. The partnership aims to enhance the financial viability of water infrastructure projects in Africa by making more public and private capital accessible for water-related infrastructure projects and encouraging and supporting African governments to invest in water governance through capacity building. The Africa-EU Water Partnership Programme is financed by the European Commission and project implementation is assigned to SIWI.

The African Development Bank and DFIs are expected to provide significant debt financing.

Commercial finance

Private investors to be determined.

Challenge

Water supply services within the Songwe River Basin in Tanzania and Malawi are in a poor state and experience challenges due to mismanagement and ageing water supply infrastructure. Additionally, new tariff regimes that improve the financial viability of the water service providers are challenging to introduce. Currently, 80% of the basin's population are classified as rural poor, with 30–50% lacking access to a safe water supply and 75% without access to electricity.

Solution

The governments of Tanzania and Malawi are currently jointly engaged in the implementation of the Songwe River Basin Development Programme (SRBDP), a 10-year programme with integrated industrial irrigation, water supply, and hydropower schemes, which jointly aim to enhance food and energy security for the basin communities in the context of the overall socio-economic development of the countries. Under the SRBDP, water supply projects for small towns around Kasumulu (Tanzania) and Songwe (Malawi) will be implemented, tapping water from the Lower Songwe dam reservoir after producing hydropower (180.2 MW). The Irrigation and Drainage scheme participants will be required to pay a fee for water provided from the new dam through the canals being planned. In collaboration with the Climate Resilient Infrastructure Development Facility, the Africa-EU Water Partnership Programme being implemented by SIWI is supporting the Songwe River Basin Commission to mobilise blended financing for the SRBDP.

SIWI is working with the SRBDP to develop a commercially sound business model for the agri-businesses that will underpin the irrigation schemes along the Songwe River. At the same time, the Climate Resilient Infrastructure Development Facility supports the project preparation of the water supply to Kasumulu and Songwe. With the socially oriented components having limited commercial potential, the bankability of the project rests on the revenue generating capacity of the lower dam and the associated hydropower plant and water supply. To improve the financial viability of the project, a blended finance approach will be used that would involve significant concessional debt from Development Finance Institutions (DFIs) and/or Multilateral Development Banks (MDBs), equity from the governments of Malawi and Tanzania, as well as commercial debt and equity from private investors. Originally planned as a PPP, in April 2019, the two governments agreed to finance the Lower Songwe Dam and hydropower plant through soft loans from financiers instead.

Dependent upon the construction of the dam and hydropower plant, a mix of grant funding and concessional debt from DFIs could meet the capital expenditure needs of the irrigation scheme and a nominal levy to fund the operational and recapitalisation costs of the scheme. The two irrigation schemes totalling 6 200 Ha will benefit farmers operating in the area with the ability to farm in two season per year leading to increased crop yield and revenues. There is therefore an opportunity for private sector investment in the agri-business sector. The positive economic and social viability of the irrigation schemes enhances the possibility of securing concessional debt finance for the capital cost of the project, with grants from development partners targeting the social projects.

Impact

The project is currently in the planning stage so the impact of the proposed development plan are as yet unknown.

Landscape-based blended financing approaches in the Kafue River Basin

Development finance

The World Wide Fund for Nature (WWF) thus far has provided technical assistance through its Bankable Water Solutions Initiative. The Government of Zambia and FMO are expected to provide financing.

Commercial finance

Anheuser-Busch InBev (AB InBev), a brewing company have committed funding for projects in the basin.

Challenge

The Kafue River Basin is an area of major ecological, industrial, and socio-economic significance for Zambia. Approximately 50% of the population of Zambia live in this area; food, water, energy, and ecosystem challenges are strongly dependent on it. According to the World Bank Group, an estimated 58% of the Zambian population lives below the poverty line and depend on ecosystems services like those provided by the Kafue Flats (World Bank, 2018[18]). The fisheries in the lower basin are also one of Zambia's most productive, supplying both urban and rural markets. Water resources management in the Kafue Flats is the cornerstone of economic activity which has an estimated GDP effect of USD 5.1 billion (WWF, 2018[19]).

There are several interlinked challenges that the basin faces going forward. The planned expansion of hydropower power plants, which will represent half of Zambia's electricity generation, will at the same time affect livelihoods. For example, hydrological processes such as annual flooding are critical in the regeneration of fish populations, while a receding flood line is an important area for grazing cattle. Planned agricultural expansion and increased water abstraction, which irrigates sugar (among other crops) as a domestic and export crop will impact water resource management. By 2011, the total area under sugarcane in the Kafue flats has grown over the past decade (currently at 27 054 ha compared to 16 140 ha in 2003). In addition, the water supply to the capital, Lusaka is predominantly from groundwater (which is already under stress) and more will need to be abstracted from the Kafue Basin. The groundwater supply and the rate of expansion of municipal services is not sufficient to keep pace with population growth. This has led to increased unplanned settlements, use of septic tanks and industrial waste seepage into the karstic geology.

Solution

The current trade-offs in the basin hence require landscape investment prototypes that will aim at a positive net impact on the landscape and ensured sustained growth. WWF has partnered with the Zambian government, private sector firms, and the Dutch development finance institution FMO to tackle this challenge in a landscape that is critical for the Zambian economy. The Kafue Flats provide a case for piloting bankable projects, because of the inter-related risks described above. Through WWF's Bankable Water Solutions Initiative, a landscape finance plan will be developed with a suite of pipeline projects that will develop water resources with a positive net impact in the Kafue Flats Landscape.

WWF has secured seed funding to execute a pre-feasibility study for an industrial wastewater treatment plant as the first step in assessing the bankability of such a project. This project would address some of the water risks faced by government and businesses.

The project has also attracted funding from AB InBev, which have a direct interest in the supply system risks/reliability for Lusaka of their own operations and their customers' wellbeing, as well as the sugar supply chain. This funding will enable WWF to further flesh out the landscape finance plan as well as to investigate the institutional and financial requirements at national level to properly execute bankable projects. An illustrative schematic of how such a plan could combine different investments across the landscape in provided in Figure A D.7.

Figure A D.7. Schematic of proposed blended finance projects that will have a net positive impact on the Kafue Flats

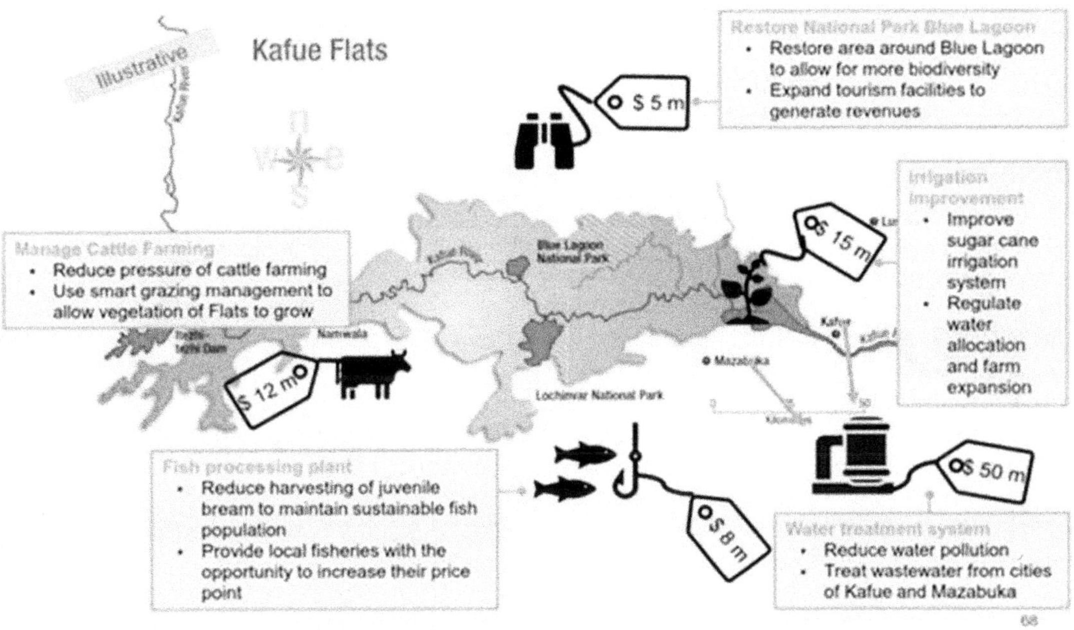

Source: (WWF, 2018[20]),

The WWF's Bankable Water Solutions Initiative has currently identified 37 projects in 24 river basins globally. The broader initiative includes a WWF enabling team, an advisory panel of experts from financial institutions, an investment platform and seed funding.

Impact

The feasibility study will provide insights into the *ex ante* view on outcomes.

References

Basile, I. and C. Neunuebel (n.d.), "Blended finance in fragile contexts", OECD, Paris. [4]

Bhavsar, D. et al. (2019), *IT enabled online monitoring systems for scheduled septic tank desludging in Maharashtra, India*, https://fsm5.susana.org/images/FSM_Conference_Materials/Tuesday/Morning/Industry/IT-enabled-online-monitoring-systems-_maharashtra_CEPT_sent.pdf (accessed on 19 August 2019). [8]

GuarantCo (2011), *GuarantCo - Portfolio - Kalangala Infrastructure Services*, https://guarantco.com/portfolio/kalangala-infrastructure-services/ (accessed on 19 August 2019). [16]

MacGeorge, R. (2009), *Lessons from Asian Experience: The Nam Theun 2 Hydroelectric Power Project (Lao PDR)*, Carec Institute, https://www.carecprogram.org/uploads/05-The-Nam-Theun-2-Hydroelectric-Power-Project-Lao-PDR.pdf (accessed on 19 August 2019). [11]

Naughton, M., N. DeSantis and A. Martoussevitch (2017), "Managing multi-purpose water infrastructure: A review of international experience", *OECD Environment Working Papers*, No. 115, OECD Publishing, Paris, https://dx.doi.org/10.1787/bbb40768-en. [12]

OECD (2018), *Making Blended Finance Work for the Sustainable Development Goals*, OECD Publishing, Paris, https://dx.doi.org/10.1787/9789264288768-en. [1]

OECD (2017), *OECD DAC Blended Finance Principles for Unlocking Commercial Finance for the Sustainable Development Goals*, https://www.oecd.org/dac/financing-sustainable-development/development-finance-topics/OECD-Blended-Finance-Principles.pdf (accessed on 6 August 2018). [5]

OECD/UNCDF (2019), *Blended Finance in the Least Developed Countries 2019*, OECD Publishing, Paris, https://dx.doi.org/10.1787/1c142aae-en. [2]

The Latin American Water Funds Partnership (2018), *IMPACTS - Fondos de Agua*, http://waterfunds.org/esp/impacts/ (accessed on 25 April 2019). [15]

TNC (2011), *Water Funds Conserving green infrastructure: A guide for design, creation and operation*, https://waterfundstoolbox.org/ (accessed on 25 April 2019). [14]

UNCDF (2018), *Blended Finance in the Least Developed Countries*, New York, https://www.uncdf.org/bfldcs/home (accessed on 28 May 2019). [3]

UNEP (2015), *WASTEWATER MANAGEMENT PLATFORMS FOR THE WIDER CARIBBEAN REGION*, http://cep.unep.org/publications-and-resources/technical-reports/cep_tr_85-en.pdf/@@download/file/CEP_TR_85-en.pdf (accessed on 8 July 2019). [7]

Valahu, P. (2015), *Kalangala (Uganda) Infrastructure Services and Renewables Projects-Transforming Bugala Island's Infrastructure*, OECD/WTO Aid for Trade Stories, https://www.oecd.org/aidfortrade/casestories/CaseStory2015_99_Uganda_EconomicInfrastructure.pdf (accessed on 19 August 2019). [17]

WHO/UNICEF (2019), *Data | JMP*, https://washdata.org/data (accessed on 8 July 2019). [6]

WHO/UNICEF (2017), *Progress on Drinking Water, Sanitation and Hygiene Update and SDG Baselines 2017*, https://www.who.int/mediacentre/news/releases/2017/launch-version-report-jmp-water-sanitation-hygiene.pdf (accessed on 14 August 2019). [21]

World Bank (2018), *Implementation Completion and Results Report: Nam Theun 2 Social and Evironment Project*, http://documents.worldbank.org/curated/en/134811549388324604/pdf/p049290-icr-01302019-636846554068325875.pdf (accessed on 25 April 2019). [10]

World Bank (2018), *Zambia Overview*, https://www.worldbank.org/en/country/zambia/overview (accessed on 14 August 2019). [18]

World Bank (2016), *Blended Financing for the Expansion of the As-Samra Wastewater Treatment Plant in Jordan Summary Overview*, http://documents.worldbank.org/curated/en/959621472041167619/pdf/107976-Jordan.pdf (accessed on 31 July 2019). [9]

World Bank (2010), *Doing a Dam Better: The Lao People's Democratic Republic and the Story of Nam Theun 2*, https://openknowledge.worldbank.org/bitstream/handle/10986/2540/584400PUB0ID161Better09780821369852.pdf?sequence=1&isAllowed=y (accessed on 19 August 2019). [13]

WWF (2018), *Banking on financial institutions to save our basin*, https://d2ouvy59p0dg6k.cloudfront.net/downloads/banking_of_financial_solutions_to_save_our_basins_1_1.pdf (accessed on 19 August 2019). [20]

WWF (2018), *Water Situational Analysis of the Lower Kafue Basin*, http://awsassets.panda.org/downloads/water_situational_analysis_of_the_lower_kafue_basin.pdf (accessed on 14 August 2019). [19]

Notes

[1] To complement this, the Government of Jordan funded a conveyance pipeline to carry high-quality treated wastewater to the Jordan Valley for use in agricultural production.

[2]EAIF is a member of PIDG that mobilises public and private funds to lend to public and private infrastructure projects in Sub-Saharan Africa.

ORGANISATION FOR ECONOMIC CO-OPERATION AND DEVELOPMENT

The OECD is a unique forum where governments work together to address the economic, social and environmental challenges of globalisation. The OECD is also at the forefront of efforts to understand and to help governments respond to new developments and concerns, such as corporate governance, the information economy and the challenges of an ageing population. The Organisation provides a setting where governments can compare policy experiences, seek answers to common problems, identify good practice and work to co-ordinate domestic and international policies.

The OECD member countries are: Australia, Austria, Belgium, Canada, Chile, the Czech Republic, Denmark, Estonia, Finland, France, Germany, Greece, Hungary, Iceland, Ireland, Israel, Italy, Japan, Korea, Latvia, Lithuania, Luxembourg, Mexico, the Netherlands, New Zealand, Norway, Poland, Portugal, the Slovak Republic, Slovenia, Spain, Sweden, Switzerland, Turkey, the United Kingdom and the United States. The European Union takes part in the work of the OECD.

OECD Publishing disseminates widely the results of the Organisation's statistics gathering and research on economic, social and environmental issues, as well as the conventions, guidelines and standards agreed by its members.

OECD PUBLISHING, 2, rue André-Pascal, 75775 PARIS CEDEX 16
ISBN 978-92-64-76737-9 – 2019

www.ingramcontent.com/pod-product-compliance
Ingram Content Group UK Ltd.
Pitfield, Milton Keynes, MK11 3LW, UK
UKHW051505290926
15471UKWH00008B/1429

9 789264 767379